ISBN 978-1-331-00434-9
PIBN 10132329

1 MONTH OF
FREE
READING

at

www.ForgottenBooks.com

By purchasing this book you are eligible for one month membership to ForgottenBooks.com, giving you unlimited access to our entire collection of over 1,000,000 titles via our web site and mobile apps.

To claim your free month visit:

www.forgottenbooks.com/free132329

English
Français
Deutsche
Italiano
Español
Português

www.forgottenbooks.com

Mythology Photography **Fiction** Fishing Christianity **Art** Cooking Essays Buddhism Freemasonry Medicine **Biology** Music **Ancient Egypt** Evolution Carpentry Physics Dance Geology **Mathematics** Fitness Shakespeare **Folklore** Yoga Marketing **Confidence** Immortality Biographies Poetry **Psychology** Witchcraft Electronics Chemistry History **Law** Accounting **Philosophy** Anthropology Alchemy Drama Quantum Mechanics Atheism Sexual Health **Ancient History** **Entrepreneurship** Languages Sport Paleontology Needlework Islam **Metaphysics** Investment Archaeology Parenting Statistics Criminology **Motivational**

VERSES.

By SUSAN COOLIDGE.

BOSTON:

ROBERTS BROTHERS.

1890.

UNIVERSITY PRESS:
JOHN WILSON AND SON, CAMBRIDGE.

TO J. H. AND E. W. H.

Nourished by peaceful suns and gracious dew,
Your sweet youth budded and your sweet lives grew,
And all the world seemed rose-beset for you.

The rose of beauty was your mutual dower,
The stainless rose of love, an early flower,
The stately blooms of ease and wealth and power.

And treading thus on pathways flower-bestrewn,
It well might be, that, cold and careless grown,
You both had lived for your own joys alone.

But, holding all these fair things as in trust,
Gently you walked, still scattering on the dust
Of harder roads, which others tread, and must, —

Your heritage of brightness, not a ray
Of noontide sought you out, but straight away
You caught and halved it with some darker day :

And as the sweet saint's loaves were turned, 't is said,
To roses, so your roses turned to bread,
That hungering souls and weary might be fed.

Dear friends, my poor words do but paint you wrong,
Nor can I utter, in one trivial song,
The goodness I have honored for so long.

Only this leaf, a single petal flung,
One chord from a full harmony unsung,
May speak the life-long love that lacks a tongue.

CONTENTS.

———◆———

CONTENTS.

3

PRELUDE.

POEMS are heavenly things,
  And only souls with wings
    May reach them where they grow,
May pluck and bear below,
Feeding the nations thus
With food all glorious.

Verses are not of these;
They bloom on earthly trees,
Poised on a low-hung stem,
And those may gather them
Who cannot fly to where
The heavenly gardens are.

So I by devious ways
Have pulled some easy sprays

PRELUDE.

From the down-dropping bough
Which all may reach, and now
I knot them, bud and leaf,
Into a rhyméd sheaf.

Not mine the pinion strong
To win the nobler song ;
I only cull and bring
A hedge-row offering
Of berry, flower, and brake,
If haply some may take.

VERSES.

COMMISSIONED.

WHAT can I do for thee, Beloved,
  Whose feet so little while ago
  Trod the same way-side dust with mine,
And now up paths I do not know
  Speed, without sound or sign?

What can I do? The perfect life
  All fresh and fair and beautiful
  Has opened its wide arms to thee;
Thy cup is over-brimmed and full;
  Nothing remains for me.

I used to do so many things, —
  Love thee and chide thee and caress;
  Brush little straws from off thy way,
Tempering with my poor tenderness
  The heat of thy short day.

Not much, but very sweet to give;
  And it is grief of griefs to bear
  That all these ministries are o'er,
And thou, so happy, Love, elsewhere,
  Never can need me more : —

And I can do for thee but this
  (Working on blindly, knowing not
  If I may give thee pleasure so) :
Out of my own dull, burdened lot
  I can arise, and go

To sadder lives and darker homes,
  A messenger, dear heart, from thee
  Who wast on earth a comforter;
And say to those who welcome me,
  I am sent forth by her.

Feeling the while how good it is
  To do thy errands thus, and think
  It may be, in the blue, far space,
Thou watchest from the heaven's brink, —
  A smile upon my face.

And when the day's work ends with day,
   And star-eyed evening, stealing in,
   Waves a cool hand to flying noon,
And restless, surging thoughts begin,
   Like sad bells out of tune,

I 'll pray : " Dear Lord, to whose great love
   Nor bound nor limit line is set,
   Give to my darling, I implore,
Some new sweet joy not tasted yet,
   For I can give no more."

And with the words my thoughts shall climb
   With following feet the heavenly stair
   Up which thy steps so lately sped,
And, seeing thee so happy there,
   · Come back half comforted.

THE CRADLE TOMB IN WESTMINSTER ABBEY.

A LITTLE, rudely sculptured bed,
  With shadowing folds of marble lace,
And quilt of marble, primly spread
  And folded round a baby's face.

Smoothly the mimic coverlet,
  With royal blazonries bedight,
Hangs, as by tender fingers set
  And straightened for the last good-night.

And traced upon the pillowing stone
  A dent is seen, as if to bless
The quiet sleep some grieving one
  Had leaned, and left a soft impress.

It seems no more than yesterday
  Since the sad mother down the stair
And down the long aisle stole away,
  And left her darling sleeping there.

But dust upon the cradle lies,
  And those who prized the baby so,
And laid her down to rest with sighs,
  Were turned to dust long years ago.

Above the peaceful pillowed head
  Three centuries brood, and strangers peep
And wonder at the carven bed, —
  But not unwept the baby's sleep,

For wistful mother-eyes are blurred
  With sudden mists, as lingerers stay,
And the old dusts are roused and stirred
  By the warm tear-drops of to-day.

Soft, furtive hands caress the stone,
  And hearts, o'erleaping place and age,
Melt into memories, and own
  A thrill of common parentage.

Men die, but sorrow never dies ;
  The crowding years divide in vain,
And the wide world is knit with ties
  Of common brotherhood in pain ;

Of common share in grief and loss,
    And heritage in the immortal bloom
Of Love, which, flowering round its cross,
    Made beautiful a baby's tomb.

"OF SUCH AS I HAVE."

OVE me for what I am, Love. Not for sake
Of some imagined thing which I might be,
Some brightness or some goodness not in me,
Born of your hope, as dawn to eyes that wake
Imagined morns before the morning break.
If I, to please you (whom I fain would please),
Reset myself like new key to old tune,
Chained thought, remodelled action, very soon
My hand would slip from yours, and by degrees
The loving, faulty friend, so close to-day,
Would vanish, and another take her place, —
A stranger with a stranger's scrutinies,
A new regard, an unfamiliar face.
Love me for what I am, then, if you may ;
But, if you cannot, — love me either way.

A PORTRAIT.

ALL sweet and various things do lend themselves
    And blend and intermix in her rare soul,
  As chorded notes, which were untuneful else,
    Clasp each the other in a perfect whole.

Within her spirit, dawn, all dewy-pearled,
    Seems held and folded in by golden noons,
While past the sunshine gleams a further world
    Of deep star-spaces and mysterious moons.

Like widths of blowing ocean wet with spray,
    Like breath of early blooms at morning caught,
Like cool airs on the cheek of heated day,
    Come the fair emanations of her thought.

Her movement, like the curving of a vine,
    Seems an unerring accident of grace,
And like a flower's the subtle change and shine
    And meaning of her brightly tranquil face.

And like a tree, unconscious of her shade,
   She spreads her helpful branches everywhere
For wandering bird or bee, nor is afraid
   Too many guests shall crowd to harbor there.

For she is kinder than all others are,
   And weak things, sad things, gather where she dwells,
To reach and taste her strength and drink of her,
   As thirsty creatures of clear water-wells.

Why vex with words where words are poor and vain?
   In one brief sentence lies the riddle's key,
Which those who love her read and read again,
   Finding each time new meanings: *She is she!*

2

WHEN ?

F I were told that I must die to-morrow,
That the next sun
Which sinks should bear me past all fear and
sorrow
For any one,
All the fight fought, all the short journey through :
What should I do ?

I do not think that I should shrink or falter,
But just go on,
Doing my work, nor change, nor seek to alter
Aught that is gone ;
But rise and move and love and smile and pray
For one more day.

And, lying down at night for a last sleeping,
Say in that ear
Which hearkens ever : " Lord, within Thy keeping
How should I fear?
And when to-morrow brings Thee nearer still,
Do Thou Thy will."

I might not sleep for awe ; but peaceful, tender,
    My soul would lie
All the night long ; and when the morning splendor
    Flushed o'er the sky,
I think that I could smile — could calmly say,
    " It is His day."

But, if instead a hand from the blue yonder
    Held out a scroll,
On which my life was writ, and I with wonder
    Beheld unroll
To a long century's end its mystic clew,
    What should I do?

What *could* I do, O blessed Guide and Master,
    Other than this :
Still to go on as now, not slower, faster,
    Nor fear to miss
The road, although so very long it be,
    While led by Thee?

Step after step, feeling Thee close beside me,
    Although unseen,

Through thorns, through flowers, whether the tempest
        hide Thee,
      Or heavens serene,
Assured Thy faithfulness cannot betray,
      Thy love decay.

I may not know, my God; no hand revealeth
      Thy counsels wise;
Along the path a deepening shadow stealeth,
      No voice replies
To all my questioning thought, the time to tell,
      And it is well.

Let me keep on, abiding and unfearing
      Thy will always,
Through a long century's ripening fruition,
      Or a short day's.
Thou canst not come too soon; and I can wait
      If thou come late.

ON THE SHORE.

THE punctual tide draws up the bay,
      With ripple of wave and hiss of spray,
      And the great red flower of the light-house tower
Blooms on the headland far away.

Petal by petal its fiery rose
Out of the darkness buds and grows;
A dazzling shape on the dim, far cape,
      A beckoning shape as it comes and goes.

A moment of bloom, and then it dies
On the windy cliff 'twixt the sea and skies.
The fog laughs low to see it go,
      And the white waves watch it with cruel eyes.

Then suddenly out of the mist-cloud dun,
As touched and wooed by unseen sun,
Again into sight bursts the rose of light
      And opens its petals one by one.

-Ah, the storm may be wild and the sea be strong,
  And man is weak and the darkness long,
But while blossoms the flower on the light-house tower
  There still is place for a smile and a song.

AMONG THE LILIES.

HE stood among the lilies
    In sunset's brightest ray,
Among the tall June lilies,
    As stately fair as they ;
And I, a boyish lover then,
Looked once, and, lingering, looked again,
    And life began that day.

She sat among the lilies,
    My sweet, all lily-pale ;
The summer lilies listened,
    I whispered low my tale.
O golden anthers, breathing balm,
. O hush of peace, O twilight calm,
    Did you or I prevail?

She lies among the lily-snows,
    Beneath the wintry sky ;

All round her and about her
The buried lilies lie.
They will awake at touch of Spring,
And she, my fair and flower-like thing,
In spring-time — by and by.

NOVEMBER.

DRY leaves upon the wall,
Which flap like rustling wings and seek escape,
A single frosted cluster on the grape
    Still hangs — and that is all.

    It hangs forgotten quite, —
Forgotten in the purple vintage-day,
Left for the sharp and cruel frosts to slay,
    The daggers of the night.

    It knew the thrill of spring ;
It had its blossom-time, its perfumed noons ;
Its pale-green spheres were rounded to soft runes
    Of summer's whispering.

    Through balmy morns of May ;
Through fragrances of June and bright July,
And August, hot and still, it hung on high
    And purpled day by day.

Of fair and mantling shapes,
No braver, fairer cluster on the tree ;
And what then is this thing has come to thee
    Among the other grapes,

Thou lonely tenant of the leafless vine,
Granted the right to grow thy mates beside,
To ripen thy sweet juices, but denied
    Thy place among the wine?

Ah ! we are dull and blind.
The riddle is too hard for us to guess
The why of joy or of unhappiness,
    Chosen or left behind.

But everywhere a host
Of lonely lives shall read their type in thine :
Grapes which may never swell the tale of wine,
    Left out to meet the frost.

EMBALMED.

THIS is the street and the dwelling,
  Let me count the houses o'er;
    Yes, — one, two, three from the corner,
And the house that I love makes four.

That is the very window
  Where I used to see her head
Bent over book or needle,
  With ivy garlanded.

And the very loop of the curtain,
  And the very curve of the vine,
Were full of the grace and the meaning
  Which was hers by some right divine.

I began to be glad at the corner,
  And all the way to the door
My heart outran my footsteps,
  And frolicked and danced before,

In haste for the words of welcome,
    The voice, the repose and grace,
And the smile, like a benediction,
    Of that beautiful, vanished face.

Now I pass the door, and I pause not,
    And I look the other way ;
But ever, a waft of fragrance,
    Too subtle to name or stay,

Comes the thought of the gracious presence
    Which made that past time sweet,
And still to those who remember,
    Embalms the house and the street,

Like the breath from some vase, now empty
    Of a flowery shape unseen,
Which follows the path of its lover,
    To tell where a rose has been.

GINEVRA DEGLI AMIERI.

A STORY OF OLD FLORENCE.

O it is come !   The doctor's glossy smile
Deceives me not.   I saw him shake his head,
Whispering, and heard poor Giulia sob without,
As, slowly creaking, he went down the stair.
Were they afraid that I should be afraid?
I, who had died once and been laid in tomb?
They need not.

    Little one, look not so pale.
I am not raving.   Ah ! you never heard
The story.   Climb up there upon the bed :
Sit close, and listen.   After this one day
I shall not tell you stories any more.

How old are you, my rose?   What ! almost twelve?
Almost a woman?   Scarcely more than that

Was your fair mother when she bore her bud ;
And scarcely more was I when, long years since,
I left my father's house, a bride in May.
You know the house, beside St. Andrea's church,
Gloomy and rich, which stands, and seems to frown
On the Mercato, humming at its base ;
And hold on high, out of the common reach,
The lilies and carved shields above its door ;
And, higher yet, to catch and woo the sun,
A little *loggia* set against the sky ?
That was my play-place ever as a child ;
And with me used to play a kinsman's son,
Antonio Rondinelli.   Ah, dear days !
Two happy things we were, with none to chide
Or hint that life was anything but play.

Sudden the play-time ended.   All at once
"You must be wed," they told me.   "What is wed ?"
I asked ; but with the word I bent my brow,
Let them put on the garland, smiled to see
The glancing jewels tied about my neck ;
And so, half-pleased, half-puzzled, was led forth
By my grave husband, older than my sire.

O the long years that followed ! It would seem
That the sun never shone in all those years,
Or only with a sudden, troubled glint
Flashed on Antonio's curls, as he went by
Doffing his cap, with eyes of wistful love
Raised to my face, — my conscious, woful face.
Were we so much to blame? Our lives had twined
Together, none forbidding, for so long.
They let our childish fingers drop the seed,
Unhindered, which should ripen to tall grain ;
They let the firm, small roots tangle and grow,
Then rent them, careless that it hurt the plant.
I loved Antonio, and he loved me.

Life was all shadow, but it was not sin !
I loved Antonio ; but I kept me pure,
Not for my husband's sake, but for the sake
Of him, my first-born child, my little child,
Mine for a few short weeks, whose touch, whose look
Thrilled all my soul and thrills it to this day.
I loved ; but, hear me swear, I kept me pure !
(Remember that, Madonna, when I come
Before thy throne to-morrow. Be not stern,
Or gaze upon me with reproachful look,

Making my little angel hide his face
And weep, while all the others turn glad eyes
Rejoicing on their mothers.)

                  It was hard
To sit in darkness while the rest had light,
To move to discords when the rest had song,
To be so young and never to have lived.
I bore, as women bear, until one day
Soul said to flesh, " This I endure no more,"
And with the word uprose, tore clay apart,
And what was blank before grew blanker still.

It was a fever, so the leeches said.
I had been dead so long, I did not know
The difference, or heed. Oil on my breast,
The garments of the grave about me wrapped,
They bore me forth, and laid me in the tomb,
The rich and beautiful and dreadful tomb,
Where all the buried Amieris lie,
Beneath the Duomo's black and towering shade.

Open the curtain, child. Yes, it is night.
It was night then, when I awoke to feel
That deadly chill, and see by ghostly gleams

Of moonlight, creeping through the grated door,
The coffins of my fathers all about.
Strange, hollow clamors rang and echoed back,
As, struggling out of mine, I dropped and fell.
With frantic strength I beat upon the grate.
It yielded to my touch.   Some careless hand
Had left the bolt half-slipped.   My father swore
Afterward, with a curse, he would make sure
Next time.   *Next time.*   That hurts me even now !

Dead or alive I issued, scarce sure which.
High overhead Giotto's tower soared ;
Behind, the Duomo rose all white and black ;
Then pealed a sudden jargoning of bells,
And down the darkling street I wildly fled,
Led by a little, cold, and wandering moon,
Which seemed as lonely and as lost as I.
I had no aim, save to reach warmth and light
And human touch ; but still my witless steps
Led to my husband's door, and there I stopped,
By instinct, knocked, and called.

                        A window oped.
A voice — 't was his — demanded : " Who is there ? "
" 'T is I, Ginevra."   Then I heard the tone

Change into horror, and he prayed aloud
And called upon the saints, the while I urged,
" O, let me in, Francesco ; let me in l
I am so cold, so frightened, let me in l "
Then, with a crash, the window was shut fast ;
And, though I cried and beat upon the door
And wailed aloud, no other answer came.

Weeping, I turned away, and feebly strove
Down the hard distance towards my father's house.
" They will have pity and will let me in,"
I thought.   " They loved me and will let me in."
Cowards !   At the high window overhead
They stood and trembled, while I plead and prayed :
" I am your child, Ginevra.   Let me in !
I am not dead.   In mercy, let me in ! "
" The holy saints forbid ! " declared my sire.
My mother sobbed and vowed whole pounds of wax
To St. Eustachio, would he but remove
This fearful presence from her door.   Then sharp
Came click of lock, and a long tube was thrust
From out the window, and my brother cried,
" Spirit or devil, go ! or else I fire ! "

Where should I go? Back to the ghastly tomb
And the cold coffined ones? Up the long street,
Wringing my hands and sobbing low, I went.
My feet were bare and bleeding from the stones;
My hands were bleeding too; my hair hung loose
Over my shroud. So wild and strange a shape
Saw never Florence since. The people call
That street through which I walked and wrung my hands
" Street of the Dead One," even to this day.
The sleeping houses stood in midnight black,
And not a soul was in the streets but I.

At last I saw a flickering point of light
High overhead, in a dim window set.
I had lain down to die; but at the sight
I rose, crawled on, and with expiring strength
Knocked, sank again, and knew not even then
It was Antonio's door by which I lay.

A window opened, and a voice called out:
" *Qui è ?* " " I am Ginevra." And I thought,
" Now he will fall to trembling, like the rest,
And bid me hence." But, lo ! a moment more
The bolts were drawn, and arms whose very touch

Was life, lifted and clasped and bore me in.
" O ghost or angel of my buried love,
I know not, care not which, be welcome here !
Welcome, thrice welcome, to this heart of mine ! "
I heard him say, and then I heard no more.

It was high noontide when I woke again,
To hear fierce voices wrangling by my bed, —
My father's and my husband's ; for, with dawn,
Gathering up valor, they had sought the tomb,
Had found me gone, and tracked my bleeding feet
Over the pavement to Antonio's door.
Dead, they cared nothing ; living, I was theirs.
Hot raged the quarrel ; then came Justice in,
And to the court we swept — I in my shroud —
To try the cause.

           This was the verdict given :
" A woman who has been to burial borne,
Made fast and left and locked in with the dead ;
Who at her husband's door has stood and plead
For entrance, and has heard her prayer denied ;
Who from her father's house is urged and chased,
Must be adjudged as dead in law and fact.

The Court pronounces the defendant — dead !
She can resume her former ties at will,
Or may renounce them, if such be her will.
She is no more a daughter, or a spouse,
Unless she choose, and is set free to form
New ties, if so she choose."

                O, blessed words !
That very day we knelt before the priest,
My love and I, were wed, and life began.

Child of my child, child of Antonio's child,
Bend down and let me kiss your wondering face.
'T is a strange tale to tell a rose like you.
But time is brief, and, had I told you not,
Haply the story would have met your ears
From them, the Amieri, my own blood,
Now turned to gall, whose foul and bitter lips
Will wag with lies when once my lips are dumb.
(Pardon me, Virgin.   I was gentle once,
And thou hast seen my wrongs.   Thou wilt forgive.)
Now go, my dearest.   When they wake thee up,
To tell thee I am dead, be not too sad.
I, who have died once, do not fear to die.

GINEVRA DEGLI AMIERI.

Sweet was that waking, sweeter will be this.
Close to Heaven's gate my own Antonio sits
Waiting, and, spite of all the Frati say,
I know I shall not stand long at that gate,
Or knock and be refused an entrance there,
For he will start up when he hears my voice,
The saints will smile, and he will open quick.
Only a night to part me from that joy.
Jesu Maria ! let the dawning come.

EASTER LILIES.

DARLINGS of June and brides of summer sun,
   Chill pipes the stormy wind, the skies are drear ;
Dull and despoiled the gardens every one :
     What do you here ?

We looked to see your gracious blooms arise
   Mid soft and wooing airs in gardens green,
Where venturesome brown bees and butterflies
     Should hail you queen.

Here is no bee nor glancing butterfly ;
   They fled on rapid wings before the snow :
Your sister lilies laid them down to die,
     Long, long ago.

And here, amid the slowly dropping rain,
   We keep our Easter feast, with hearts whose care
Mars the high cadence of each lofty strain,
     Each thankful prayer.

But not a shadow dims your joyance sweet,
　No baffled hope or memory darkly clad ;
You lay your whiteness at the Lord's dear feet,
　　　And are all glad.

O coward soul ! arouse thee and draw near,
　Led by these fragrant acolytes to-day !
Let their sweet confidence rebuke thy fear,
　　　Thy cold delay.

Come with thy darkness to the healing light,
　Come with thy bitter, which shall be made sweet,
And lay thy soil beside the lilies white,
　　　At His dear feet !

EBB-TIDE.

ONG reaches of wet grasses sway
Where ran the sea but yesterday,
And white-winged boats at sunset drew
To anchor in the crimsoning blue.
The boats lie on the grassy plain,
Nor tug nor fret at anchor chain ;
Their errand done, their impulse spent,
Chained by an alien element,
With sails unset they idly lie,
Though morning beckons brave and nigh ;
Like wounded birds, their flight denied,
They lie, and long and wait the tide.

About their keels, within the net
Of tough grass fibres green and wet,
A myriad thirsty creatures, pent
In sorrowful imprisonment,
Await the beat, distinct and sweet,
Of the white waves' returning feet.

My soul their vigil joins, and shares
A nobler discontent than theirs ;
Athirst like them, I patiently
Sit listening beside the sea,
And still the waters outward glide :
When is the turning of the tide ?

Come, pulse of God ; come, heavenly thrill !
We wait thy coming, — and we will.
The world is vast, and very far
Its utmost verge and boundaries are ;
But thou hast kept thy word to-day
In India and in dim Cathay,
And the same mighty care shall reach
Each humblest rock-pool of this beach.
The gasping fish, the stranded keel,
This dull dry soul of mine, shall feel
Thy freshening touch, and, satisfied,
Shall drink the fulness of the tide.

FLOOD–TIDE.

ALL night the thirsty beach has listening lain,
    With patience dumb,
Counting the slow, sad moments of her pain ;
    Now morn has come,
And with the morn the punctual tide again.

I hear the white battalions down the bay
    Charge with a cheer ;
The sun's gold lances prick them on their way, —
    They plunge, they rear, —
Foam-plumed and snowy-pennoned, they are here !

The rouséd shore, her bright hair backward blown,
    Stands on the verge
And waves a smiling welcome, beckoning on
    The flying surge,
While round her feet, like doves, the billows crowd and
      urge.

Her glad lips quaff the salt, familiar wine ;
       Her spent urns fill ;
All hungering creatures know the sound, the sign, —
       Quiver and thrill,
With glad expectance crowd and banquet at their will.

I, too, the rapt contentment join and share ;
       My tide is full ;
There is new happiness in earth, in air :
       All beautiful
And fresh the world but now so bare and dull.

But while we raise the cup of bliss so high,
       Thus satisfied,
Another shore beneath a sad, far sky
       Waiteth her tide,
And thirsts with sad complainings still denied.

On earth's remotest bound she sits and waits
       In doubt and pain ;
Our joy is signal for her sad estates ;
       Like dull refrain
Marring our song, her sighings rise in vain.

To each his turn — the ebb-tide and the flood,
        The less, the more —
God metes his portions justly out, I know ;
        But still before
My mind forever floats that pale and grieving shore.

A YEAR.

SHE has been just a year in Heaven.
   Unmarked by white moon or gold sun,
   By stroke of clock or clang of bell,
Or shadow lengthening on the way,
In the full noon and perfect day,
In Safety's very citadel,
The happy hours have sped, have run ;
And, rapt in peace, all pain forgot,
She whom we love, her white soul shriven,
Smiles at the thought and wonders not.

We have been just a year alone, —
A year whose calendar is sighs,
And dull, perpetual wishfulness,
And smiles, each covert for a tear,
And wandering thoughts, half there, half here,
And weariful attempts to guess
The secret of the hiding skies,
The soft, inexorable blue,

With gleaming hints of glory sown,
And Heaven behind, just shining through.

So sweet, so sad, so swift, so slow,
So full of eager growth and light,
So full of pain which blindly grows,
So full of thoughts which either way
Have passed and crossed and touched each day,
To us a thorn, to her a rose ;
The year so black, the year so white,
Like rivers twain their course have run ;
The earthly stream we trace and know,
But who shall paint the heavenly one ?

A year ! We gather up our powers,
Our lamps we consecrate and trim ;
Open all windows to the day,
And welcome every heavenly air.
We will press forward and will bear,
Having this word to cheer the way :
She, storm-tossed once, is safe with Him,
Healed, comforted, content, forgiven ;
And while we count these heavy hours
Has been a year, — a year in Heaven.

TOKENS.

ACH day upon the yellow Nile, 't is said,
Joseph, the youthful ruler, cast forth wheat,
That haply, floating to his father's feet, —
The sad old father, who believed him dead, —
It might be sign in Egypt there was bread;
And thus the patriarch, past the desert sands
And scant oasis fringed with thirsty green,
Be lured toward the love that yearned unseen.
So, flung and scattered —ah ! by what dear hands ?—
On the swift-rushing and invisible tide,
Small tokens drift adown from far, fair lands,
And say to us, who in the desert bide,
"Are you athirst?   Are there no sheaves to bind?
Beloved, here is fulness ; follow on and find."

HER GOING.

SUGGESTED BY A PICTURE.

HE stood in the open door,
　　She blessed them faint and low :
　　" I must go," she said, "must go
　　Away from the light of the sun,
　　Away from you, every one ;
Must see your eyes no more, —
　　Your eyes, that love me so.

" I should not shudder thus,
　.Nor weep, nor be afraid,
　　Nor cling to you so dismayed,
　　　Could I only pierce with my eyes
　　　Where the dark, dark shadow lies ;
Where something hideous
　　Is hiding, perhaps," she said.

Then slowly she went from them,
　　Went down the staircase grim,

With trembling heart and limb ;
Her footfalls echoéd
In the silence vast and dead,
Like the notes of a requiem,
Not sung, but utteréd.

For a little way and a black
She groped as grope the blind,
Then a sudden radiance shined,
And a vision her eyelids burned ;
All joyfully she turned,
For a moment turned she back,
And smiled at those behind.

There in the shadows drear
An angel sat serene,
Of grave and tender mien,
With whitest roses crowned ;
A scythe lay on the ground,
As reaping-time were near, —
A burnished scythe and a keen.

She did not start or pale
As the angel rose and laid

His hand on hers, nor said
  A word, but beckoned on ;
  For a glorious meaning shone
On the lips that told no tale,
  And she followed him, unafraid.

Her friends wept for a space ;
  Then one said : " Be content ;
  Surely some good is meant
    For her, our Beautiful, —
    Some glorious good and full.
Did you not see her face,
  Her dear smile, as she went ? "

A LONELY MOMENT.

SIT alone in the gray,
   The snow falls thick and fast,
And never a sound have I heard all day
   But the wailing of the blast,
And the hiss and click of the snow, whirling to and fro.

There seems no living thing
   Left in the world but I ;
My thoughts fly forth on restless wing,
   And drift back wearily,
Storm-beaten, buffeted, hopeless, and almost dead.

No one there is to care ;
   Not one to even know
Of the lonely day and the dull despair
   As the hours ebb and flow,
Slow lingering, as fain to lengthen out my pain.

And I think of the monks of old,
    Each in his separate cell,
  Hearing no sound, except when tolled
    The stated convent bell.
How could they live and bear that silence everywhere?

And I think of tumbling seas,
    'Neath cruel, lonely skies ;
  And shipwrecked sailors over these
    Stretching their hungry eyes, —
Eyes dimmed with wasting tears for weary years on years, —

Pacing the hopeless sand,
    Wistful and wan and pale,
  Each foam-flash like a beckoning hand,
    Each wave a glancing sail,
And so for days and days, and still the sail delays.

I hide my eyes in vain,
    In vain I try to smile ;
  That urging vision comes again,
    The sailor on his isle,
With none to hear his cry, to help him live — or die !

And with the pang a thought
    Breaks o'er me like the sun,
Of the great listening Love which caught
    Those accents every one,
Nor lost one faintest word, but always, always heard.

The monk his vigil pale
    Could lighten with a smile,
The sailor's courage need not fail
    Upon his lonely isle ;
For there, as here, by sea or land, the pitying Lord stood
      close at hand.

O coward heart of mine !
    When storms shall beat again,
Hold firmly to this thought divine,
    As anchorage in pain :
That, lonely though thou seemest to be, the Lord is near,
      remembering thee.

COMMUNION.

HAT is it to commune?
It is when soul meets soul, and they embrace
As souls may, stooping from each separate sphere
    For a brief moment's space.

What is it to commune?
It is to lay the veil of custom by,
To be all unafraid of truth, to talk
    Face to face, eye to eye.

Not face to face, dear Lord;
That is the joy of brighter worlds to be;
And yet, Thy bidden guests about Thy board,
    We do commune with Thee.

Behind the white-robed priest
Our eyes, anointed with a sudden grace,
Dare to conjecture of a mighty guest,
    A dim belovéd Face.

And is it Thou, indeed?
And dost Thou lay Thy glory all away
To visit us, and with Thy grace to feed
　　Our hungering hearts to-day?

And can a thing so sweet,
And can such heavenly condescension be?
Ah! wherefore tarry thus our lingering feet?
　　It can be none but Thee.

There is the gracious ear
That never yet was deaf to sinner's call;
We will not linger, and we dare not fear,
　　But kneel, — and tell Thee all.

We tell Thee of our sin
Only half loathed, only half wished away,
And those clear eyes of Love that look within
　　Rebuke us, seem to say, —

" O, bought with my own blood,
Mine own, for whom my precious life I gave,
Am I so little prized, remembered, loved,
　　By those I died to save? "

And under that deep gaze
Sorrow awakes ; we kneel with eyelids wet,
And marvel, as with Peter at the gate,
That we could so forget.

We tell Thee of our care,
Of the sore burden, pressing day by day,
And in the light and pity of Thy face
The burden melts away.

We breathe our secret wish,
The importunate longing which no man may see ;
We ask it humbly, or, more restful still,
We leave it all to Thee.

And last our amulet
Of precious names we thread, and soft and low
We crave for each beloved, or near or far,
A blessing ere we go.

The thorns are turned to flowers,
All dark perplexities seem light and fair,
A mist is lifted from the heavy hours,
And Thou art everywhere.

A FAREWELL.

G O, sun, since go you must,
   The dusky evening lowers above our sky,
    Our sky which was so blue and sweetly fair;
Night is not terrible that we should sigh.
   A little darkness we can surely bear;
Will there not be more sunshine — by and by?

   · Go, rose, since go you must,
Flowerless and chill the winter draweth nigh;
   Closed are the blithe and fragrant lips which made
All summer long perpetual melody.
   Cheerless we take our way, but not afraid:
Will there not be more roses — by and by?

    Go, love, since go you must,
Out of our pain we bless you as you fly;
   The momentary heaven the rainbow lit
Was worth whole days of black and stormy sky;
   Shall we not see, as by the waves we sit,
Your bright sail winging shoreward — by and by?

Go, life, since go you must,
Uncertain guest and whimsical ally !
    All questionless you came, unquestioned go ;
What does it mean to live, or what to die ?
    Smiling we see you vanish, for we know
Somewhere is nobler living — by and by.

EBB AND FLOW.

OW easily He turns the tides !
   Just now the yellow beach was dry,
   Just now the gaunt rocks all were bare,
The sun beat hot, and thirstily
Each sea-weed waved its long brown hair,
   And bent and languished as in pain ;
Then, in a flashing moment's space,
   The white foam-feet which spurned the sand
Paused in their joyous outward race,
   Wheeled, wavered, turned them to the land,
And, a swift legionary band,
   Poured on the waiting shores again.

How easily He turns the tides !
   The fulness of my yesterday
Has vanished like a rapid dream,
   And pitiless and far away
The cool, refreshing waters gleam :
   Grim rocks of dread and doubt and pain

Rear their dark fronts where once was sea ;
   But I can smile and wait for Him
Who turns. the tides so easily,
   Fills the spent rock-pool to its brim,
And up from the horizon dim
   Leads His bright morning waves again.

ANGELUS.

OFTLY drops the crimson sun :
   Softly down from overhead,
   Drop the bell-notes, one by one,
    Melting in the melting red ;
Sign to angel bands unsleeping, —
   " Day is done, the dark is dread,
Take the world in care and keeping.

" Set the white-robed sentries close,
   Wrap our want and weariness
In the surety of repose ;
   Let the shining presences,
Bearing fragrance on their wings,
   Stand about our beds to bless,
Fright away all evil things.

" Rays of Him whose shadow pours
  Through all lives a brimming glory,
Float o'er darksome woods and moors,
  Float above the billows hoary ;
Shine, through night and storm and sin,
  Tangled fate and bitter story,
Guide the lost and wandering in ! "

Now the last red ray is gone ;
  Now the twilight shadows hie ;
Still the bell-notes, one by one,
  Send their soft voice to the sky,
Praying, as with human lip, —
  " Angels, hasten, night is nigh,
Take us to thy guardianship."

THE MORNING COMES BEFORE THE SUN.

SLOW buds the pink dawn like a rose
    From out night's gray and cloudy sheath ;
    Softly and still it grows and grows,
      Petal by petal, leaf by leaf ;
    Each sleep-imprisoned creature breaks
      Its dreamy fetters, one by one,
    And love awakes, and labor wakes, —
      The morning comes before the sun.

    What is this message from the light
      So fairer far than light can be ?
  Youth stands a-tiptoe, eager, bright,
      In haste the risen sun to see ;
    Ah ! check thy longing, restless heart,
      Count the charmed moments as they run,
    It is life's best and fairest part,
      This morning hour before the sun.

When once thy day shall burst to flower,
   When once the sun shall climb the sky,
And busy hour by busy hour,
   The urgent noontide draws anigh ;
When the long shadows creep abreast,
   To dim the happy task half done,
Thou wilt recall this pause of rest,
   This morning hush before the sun.

To each, one dawning and one dew,
   One fresh young hour is given by fate,
One rose flush on the early blue.
   Be not impatient then, but wait !
Clasp the sweet peace on earth and sky,
   By midnight angels woven and spun ;
Better than day its prophecy, —
   The morning comes before the sun.

5

LABORARE EST ORARE.

" Although St. Francesca was unwearied in her devotions, yet if, during her prayers, she was called away by her husband or any domestic duty, she would close the book cheerfully, saying that a wife and a mother, when called upon, must quit her God at the altar to find Him in her domestic affairs." — *Legends of the Monastic Orders.*

HOW infinite and sweet, Thou everywhere
        And all abounding Love, Thy service is !
    Thou liest an ocean round my world of care,
    My petty every-day ; and fresh and fair,
        Pour Thy strong tides through all my crevices,
    Until the silence ripples into prayer.

    That Thy full glory may abound, increase,
        And so Thy likeness shall be formed in me,
    I pray ; the answer is not rest or peace,
    But charges, duties, wants, anxieties,
        Till there seems room for everything but Thee,
    And never time for anything but these.

    And I should fear, but lo ! amid the press,
        The whirl and hum and pressure of my day,

I hear Thy garment's sweep, Thy seamless dress,
And close beside my work and weariness
    Discern Thy gracious form, not far away,
But very near, O Lord, to help and bless.

The busy fingers fly, the eyes may see
    Only the glancing needle which they hold,
But all my life is blossoming inwardly,
And every breath is like a litany,
    While through each labor, like a thread of gold,
Is woven the sweet consciousness of Thee.

EIGHTEEN.

A H ! grown a dim and fairy shade,
　　Dear child, who, fifteen years ago,
　　　Out of our arms escaped and fled
With swift white feet, as if afraid,
　To hide beneath the grass, the snow,
　　That sunny little head.

This is your birthday !　Fair, so fair,
　And grown to gracious maiden-height,
　　And versed in heavenly lore and ways ;
White-vested as the angels are,
　In very light of very light,
　　Somehow, somewhere, you keep the day :

With those new friends, whom " new " we call,
　But who are dearer now than we,
　　And better known by face and name :
And do they smile and say, " How tall
　The child becomes, how radiant, she
　　Who was so little when she came ! "

Darling, we count your eighteen years, —
   Fifteen in Heaven, on earth but three, —
     And try to frame you grown and wise :
But all in vain ; there still appears
   Only the child you used to be,
     Our baby with the violet eyes.

OUTWARD BOUND.

A GRIEVOUS day of wrathful winds,
   Of low-hung clouds, which scud and fly,
And drop cold rains, then lift and show
A sullen realm of upper sky.

The sea is black as night ; it roars
   From lips afoam with cruel spray,
Like some fierce, many-throated pack
   Of wolves, which scents and chases prey.

Crouched in my little wind-swept nook,
   I hear the menacing voices call,
And shudder, as above the deck
   .Topples and swings the weltering wall.

It seems a vast and restless grave,
   Insatiate, hungry, beckoning
With dreadful gesture of command
   To every free and living thing.

" O Lord," I cry, " Thou makest life
  And hope and all sweet things to be ;
Rebuke this hovering, following Death, —
  This horror never born of Thee."

A sudden gleam, the waves light up
  With radiant, momentary hues, —
Amber and shadowy pearl and gold,
  Opal and green and unknown blues, —

And, rising on the tossing walls,
  Within the foaming valleys swung,
Soft shapes of sea-birds, dimly seen,
  Flutter and float and call their young,

A moment ; then the lowering clouds
  Settle anew above the main,
The colors die, the waves rise higher,
  And night and terror rule again.

No more I see the small, dim shapes,
  So unafraid of wind and wave,
Nestling beneath the tempest's roar,
  Cradled in what I deemed a grave.

OUTWARD BOUND.

But all night long I lie and smile
 At thought of those soft folded wings,
Still trusting, with the trustful birds,
 In Him who cares for smallest things.

FROM EAST TO WEST.

THE boat cast loose her moorings;
   "Good-by" was all we said.
   "Good-by, Old World," we said with a smile,
  And never looked back as we sped,
A shining wake of foam behind,
   To the heart of the sunset red.

Heavily drove our plunging keel
  The warring waves between;
Heavily strove we night and day,
  Against the west-wind keen,
Bent, like a foe, to bar our path, —
  A foe with an awful mien.

Never a token met our eyes
  From the dear land far away;
No storm-swept bird, no drifting branch,
  To tell us where it lay.

Wearily searched we, hour by hour,
   Through the mist and the driving spray,

Till, all in a flashing moment,
   The fog-veils rent and flew,
And a blithesome south-wind caught the sails
   And whistled the cordage through,
And the stars swung low their silver lamps
   In a dome of airy blue,

And, breathed from unseen distances,
   A new and joyous air
Caressed our senses suddenly
   With a rapture fresh and rare.
" It is the breath of home ! " we cried ;
   " We feel that we are there."

O Land whose tent-roof is the dome
   Of Heaven's purest sky,
Whose mighty heart inspires the wind
   Of glad, strong liberty,
Standing upon thy sunset shore,
   Beside the waters high,

Long may thy rosy smile be bright;
   Above the ocean din
Thy young, undaunted voice be heard,
   Calling the whole world kin;
And ever be thy arms held out
   To take the storm-tossed in!

UNA.

UNA.

M Y darling once lived by my side,
   She scarcely ever went away;
   We shared our studies and our play,
Nor did she care to walk or ride
   Unless I did the same that day.

Now she is gone to some far place;
   I never see her any more,
   The pleasant play-times all are o'er;
I come from school, there is no face
   To greet me at the open door.

At first I cried all day, all night;
   I could not bear to eat or smile,
   I missed her, missed her, all the while;
The brightest day did not look bright,
   The shortest walk was like a mile.

Then some one came and told me this:
  "Your playmate is but gone from view,
  Close by your side she stands, and you
Can almost hear her breathe, and kiss
  Her soft cheek as you used to do.

"Only a little veil between, —
  A slight, thin veil; if you could see
  Past its gray folds, there she would be,
Smiling and sweet, and she would lean
  And stretch her hands out joyfully.

"All the day long, and year by year,
  She will go forward as you go;
  As you grow older, she will grow;
As you grow good, she, with her clear
  And angel eyes, will mark and know.

"Think, when you wake up every day,
  That she is standing by your bed,
  Close to the pillow where her head,
Her little curly head, once lay,
  With a 'Good-morning' smiled, not said.

" Think, when the books seem dull and tame,
   The sports no longer what they were,
   That there she sits, a shape of air,
And turns the leaf or joins the game
   With the same smile she used to wear.

" So, moving on still, hand in hand,
   One of these days your eyes will clear,
   The hiding veil will disappear,
And you will know and understand
   Just why your playmate left you here."

This made me happier, and I try
   To think each day that it may be.
   Sometimes I do so easily ;
But then again I have to cry,
   Because I want so much to *see !*

TWO WAYS TO LOVE.

" Entre deux amants il y a toujours l'un qui baise et l'autre qui tend la joue."

I.

HE says he loves me well, and I
    Believe it; in my hands, to make
Or mar, his life lies utterly,
Nor can I the strong plea deny,
    Which claims my love for his love's sake.

He says there is no face so fair
    As mine; when I draw near, his eyes
Light up; each ripple of my hair
He loves; the very cloak I wear
    He touches fondly where it lies.

And roses, roses all the way,
    Upon my path fall, strewed by him;
His tenderness by night, by day,
Keeps faithful watch to heap alway
    My cup of pleasure to the brim.

The other women, full of spite,
  Count me the happiest woman born
To be so worshipped ; I delight
To flaunt his homage in their sight, —
  For me the rose, for them its thorn.

I love him, — or I think I do ;
  Sure one *must* love what is so sweet.
He is all tender and all true,
All eloquent to plead and sue,
  All strength — though kneeling at my feet.

Yet I had visions once of yore,
  Girlish imaginings of a zest,
A possible thrill, — but why run o'er
These fancies? — idle dreams, no more ;
  I will forget them, this is best.

So let him take, — the past is past ;
  The future, with its golden key,
Into his outstretched hands I cast.
I shall love him — perhaps — at last,
  As now I love his love for me.

II.

Not as all other women may,
　Love I my Love ; he is so great,
So beautiful, I dare essay
No nearness, but in silence lay
　My heart upon his path, — and wait.

Poor heart ! its beatings are so low
　He does not heed them passing by,
Save as one heeds, where violets grow,
A fragrance, caring not to know
　Where the veiled purple buds may lie.

I sometimes think that it is dead,
　It lies so still.　I bend and lean,
Like mother over cradle-head,
Wondering if still faint breaths are shed
　Like sighs the parted lips between.
6

And then, with vivid pulse and thrill,
　　It quickens into sudden bliss
At sound of step or voice, nor will
Be hushed, although, regardless still,
　　He knows not, cares not, it is his.

I would not lift it if I could :
　　The little flame, though faint and dim
As glow-worm spark in lonely wood,
Shining where no man calls it good,
　　May one day light the path for him, —

May guide his way, or soon or late,
　　Through blinding mist or wintry rain ;
And, so content, I watch and wait.
Let others share his happier fate,
　　I only ask to share his pain !

And if some day, when passing by,
　　My dear Love should his steps arrest,
Should mark the poor heart waiting nigh,
Should know it his, should lift it, — why,
　　Patience is good, but joy is best !

AFTER-GLOW.

Y morn was all dewy rose and pearl,
　　Peace brimmed the skies, a cool and fragrant air
　　Caressed my going forth, and everywhere
The radiant webs, by hope and fancy spun,
　　Stretched shining in the sun.

Then came a noon, hot, breathless, still, —
　　No wind to visit the dew-thirsty flowers,
　　Only the dust, the road, the urging hours ;
And, pressing on, I never guessed or knew
　　That day was half-way through.

And when a pomp of purple lit the sky,
　　And sheaves of golden lances tipped with red
　　Danced in the west, wondering I gazed, and said,
" Lo, a new morning comes, my hopes to crown ! "
　　Sudden the sun dropped down

Like a great golden ball into the sea,
 Which made room, laughing, and the serried rank
 Of yellow lances flashed, and, turning, sank
After their chieftain, as he led the way,
  And all the heaven was gray.

Startled and pale, I stood to see them go ;
 Then a long, stealing shadow to me crept,
 And laid his cold hand on me, and I wept
And hid my eyes, and shivered with affright
  At thought of coming night.

But as I wept and shuddered, a warm thrill
 Smote on my sense.   I raised my eyes, and lo !
 The skies, so dim but now, were all aglow
With a new flush of tender rose and gold,
  Opening fold on fold.

Higher and higher soared the gracious beam,
 Deeper and deeper glowed the heavenly hues,
 Nor any cowering shadow could refuse
The beautiful embrace which clasped and kissed
  Its dun to amethyst.

A little longer, and the lovely light,
   Draining the last drops from its wondrous urn,
   Departed, and the swart shades in their turn,
Impatient of the momentary mirth,
     Crowded to seize the earth.

No longer do I shudder. With calm eye
   I front the night, nor wish its hours away ;
   For in that message from my banished day
I read his pledge of dawn, and soon or late
     I can endure to wait.

HOPE AND I.

OPE stood one morning by the way,
　　And stretched her fair right hand to me,
And softly whispered, " For this day
　　I 'll company with thee."

" Ah, no, dear Hope," I sighing said ;
　　" Oft have you joined me in the morn,
But when the evening came, you fled
　　And left me all forlorn.

" 'T is better I should walk alone
　　Than have your company awhile,
And then to lose it, and go on
　　For weary mile on mile."

She turned, rebuked.　I went my way,
　　But sad the sunshine seemed, and chill ;
I missed her, missed her all the day,
　　And O, I miss her still.

LEFT BEHIND.

WE started in the morning, a morning full of glee,
  All in the early morning, a goodly company ;
  And some were full of merriment, and all were
    kind and dear ;
But the others have pursued their way, and left me sitting
  here.

My feet were not so fleet as theirs, my courage soon was
  gone,
And so I lagged and fell behind, although they cried " Come
  on ! "
They cheered me and they pitied me, but one by one
  went by,
For the stronger must outstrip the weak : there is no
  remedy.

Some never looked behind, but smiled, and swiftly, hand
    in hand,
Departed with a strange sweet joy I could not understand ;
I know not by what silver streams their roses bud and
    blow,
But I am glad — O very glad — they should be happy so.

And some they went companionless, yet not alone, it
    seemed,
For there were sounds of rustling wings, and songs, — or
    else we dreamed ;
And a glow from lights invisible to us lit up the place,
And tinged, as if with glory, each dear and parting face.

So happy, happy did they look, as one by one they went,
That we, who missed them sorely, were fain to be content ;
And I, who sit the last of all, left far behind, alone,
Cannot be sorry for their sakes, but only for my own.

My eyes seek out the different paths by which they went
    away,
And oft I wish to follow, but oftener wish to stay ;
For fair as may the new things be, the farther things they
    know,
This is a pleasant resting-place, a pleasant place also.

here are flowers for the gathering, which grow my path
anear,

he skies are fair, and everywhere the sun is warm and
clear :

may have missed the wine of life, the strong wine and
the new,

ut I have my wells of water, my sips of honey-dew.

o when I turn my thoughts from those who shared my
dawn of day,

y fresh and joyous morning prime, and now are passed
away,

I can see just how sweet all is, how good, and be resigned

To sit thus in the afternoon, alone and left behind.

SAVOIR C'EST PARDONNER.

MYRIAD rivers seek the sea,
    The sea rejects not any one ;
A myriad rays of light may be
    Clasped in the compass of one sun ;
And myriad grasses, wild and free,
    Drink of the dew which faileth none.

A myriad worlds encompass ours ;
    A myriad souls our souls enclose ;
And each, its sins and woes and powers,
    The Lord He sees, the Lord He knows,
And from the Infinite Knowledge flowers
    The Infinite Pity's fadeless rose.

Lighten our darkness, Lord, most wise ;
    All-seeing One, give us to see ;
Our judgments are profanities,
    Our ignorance is cruelty,
While Thou, knowing all, dost not despise
    To pardon even such things as we.

MORNING.

WORD and thing most beautiful !
Our yesterday was cold and dull,
   Gray mists obscured the setting sun,
Its evening wept with sobbing rain ;
But to and fro, mid shrouding night,
   Some healing angel swift has run,
And all is fresh and fair again.

O, word and thing most beautiful !
The hearts, which were of cares so full,
   The tired hands, the tired feet,
So glad of night, are glad of morn, —
Where are the clouds of yesterday ?
   The world is good, the world is sweet,
And life is new and hope re-born.

O, word and thing most beautiful !
O coward soul and sorrowful,
   Which sighs to note the ebbing light
Give place to evening's shadowy gray !
   What are these things but parables, —
That darkness heals the wrongs of day,
   And dawning clears all mists of night.

O, word and thing most beautiful !
The little sleep our cares to lull,
   The long, soft dusk and then sunrise,
To waken fresh and angel fair,
   Life all renewed and cares forgot,
   Ready for Heaven's glad surprise,
So Christ, who is our Light, be there.

A BLIND SINGER.

I N covert of a leafy porch,
　　Where woodbine clings,
And roses drop their crimson leaves,
　　He sits and sings ;
With soft brown crest erect to hear,
　　And drooping wings.

Shut in a narrow cage, which bars
　　His eager flight,
Shut in the darker prison-house
　　Of blinded sight,
Alike to him are sun and stars,
　　The day, the night.

But all the fervor of high noon,
　　Hushed, fragrant, strong,

And all the peace of moonlit nights
    When nights are long,
And all the bliss of summer eves,
    Breathe in his song.

The rustle of the fresh green woods,
    The hum of bee,
The joy of flight, the perfumed waft
    Of blossoming tree,
The half-forgotten, rapturous thrill
    Of liberty, —

All blend and mix, while evermore,
    Now and again,
A plaintive, puzzled cadence comes,
    A low refrain,
Caught from some shadowy memory
    Of patient pain.

In midnight black, when all men sleep,
    My singer wakes,
And pipes his lovely melodies,
    And trills and shakes.
The dark sky bends to listen, but
    No answer makes.

O, what is joy?   In vain we grasp
    Her purple wings ;
Unwon, unwooed, she flits to dwell
    With humble things ;
She shares my sightless singer's cage,
    And so — he sings.

MARY.

HE drowsy summer in the flowering limes
    Had laid her down at ease,
Lulled by soft, sportive winds, whose tinkling
    chimes
Summoned the wandering bees
To feast, and dance, and hold high carnival
Within that vast and fragrant banquet-hall.

She stood, my Mary, on the wall below,
    Poised on light, arching feet,
And drew the long, green branches down to show
    Where hung, mid odors sweet, —
A tiny miracle to touch and view, —
The humming-bird's small nest and pearls of blue.

Fair as the summer's self she stood, and smiled,
    With eyes like summer sky,

Wistful and glad, half-matron and half-child,
    Gentle and proud and shy ;
Her sweet head framed against the blossoming bough,
She stood a moment, — and she stands there now !

'T is sixteen years since, trustful, unafraid,
    In her full noon of light,
She passed beneath the grass's curtaining shade,
    Out of our mortal sight ;
And springs and summers, bearing gifts to men,
And long, long winters have gone by since then.

And each some little gift has brought to dress
    That unforgotten bed, —
Violet, anemone, or lady's-tress,
    Or spray of berries red,
Or purpling leaf, or mantle, pure and cold,
Of winnowed snow, wrapped round it, fold on fold.

Yet still she stands, a glad and radiant shape,
    Set in the morning fair, —
That vanished morn which had such swift escape.
    I turn and see her there, —
The arch, sweet smile, the bending, graceful head ;
And, seeing thus, why do I call her dead ?

WHEN LOVE WENT.

WHAT whispered Love the day he fled?
   Ah ! this was what Love whispered :
   " You sought to hold me with a chain ;
I fly to prove such holding vain.

" You bound me burdens, and I bore
The burdens hard, the burdens sore ;
I bore them all unmurmuring,
For Love can bear a harder thing.

" You taxed me often, teased me, wept ;
I only smiled, and still I kept
Through storm and sun and night and day,
My joyous, viewless, faithful way.

" But, dear, once dearest, you and I
This day have parted company.
Love must be free to give, defer,
Himself alone his almoner.

"As free I freely poured my all,
Enslaved I spurn, renounce my thrall,
Its wages and its bitter bread."
Thus whispered Love the day he fled !

OVERSHADOWED.

" Insomuch that they brought forth the sick into the streets, and laid them on beds and couches, that at the least the shadow of Peter, passing by, might over-shadow some of them."

ID the thronged bustle of the city street,
    In the hot hush of noon,
  I wait, with folded hands and nerveless feet.
    Surely He will come soon.
  Surely the Healer will not pass me by,
  But listen to my cry.

  Long are the hours in which I lie and wait,
    Heavy the load I bear ;
  But He will come ere evening.   Soon or late
    I shall behold Him there ;
  Shall hear His dear voice, all the clangor through :
  " What wilt thou that I do?"

  " If Thou but wilt, Lord, Thou canst make me clean."
    Thus shall I answer swift.

And He will touch me, as He walks serene ;
   And I shall rise and lift
This couch, so long my prison-house of pain,
And be made whole again.

He lingers yet. But lo ! a hush, a hum.
   The multitudes press on
After some leader. Surely He is come !
   He nears me ; He is gone !
Only His shadow reached me, as He went ;
Yet here I rest content.

In that dear shadow, like some healing spell,
   A heavenly patience lay ;
Its balm of peace enwrapped me as it fell ;
   My pains all fled away, —
The weariness, the deep unrest of soul ;
I am indeed " made whole."

It is enough, Lord, though Thy face divine
   Was turned to other men.
Although no touch, no questioning voice was mine,
   Thou wilt come once again ;
And, if Thy shadow brings such bliss to me,
What must Thy presence be ?

TIME TO GO.

THEY know the time to go !
  The fairy clocks strike their inaudible hour
  In field and woodland, and each punctual flower
Bows at the signal an obedient head
      And hastes to bed.

      The pale Anemone
Glides on her way with scarcely a good-night ;
The Violets tie their purple nightcaps tight ;
Hand clasped in hand, the dancing Columbines,
      In blithesome lines,

      Drop their last courtesies,
Flit from the scene, and couch them for their rest ;
The Meadow Lily folds her scarlet vest
And hides it 'neath the Grasses' lengthening green ;
      Fair and serene,

Her sister Lily floats
On the blue pond, and raises golden eyes
To court the golden splendor of the skies, —
The sudden signal comes, and down she goes
  To find repose

  In the cool depths below.
A little later, and the Asters blue
Depart in crowds, a brave and cheery crew;
While Golden-rod, still wide awake and gay,
  Turns him away,

  Furls his bright parasol,
And, like a little hero, meets his fate.
The Gentians, very proud to sit up late,
Next follow. Every Fern is tucked and set
  'Neath coverlet,

  Downy and soft and warm.
No little seedling voice is heard to grieve
Or make complaints the folding woods beneath;
No lingerer dares to stay, for well they know
  The time to go.

Teach us your patience brave,
Dear flowers, till we shall dare to part like you,
Willing God's will, sure that his clock strikes true,
That his sweet day augurs a sweeter morrow,
With smiles, not sorrow.

GULF–STREAM.

ONELY and cold and fierce I keep my way,
   Scourge of the lands, companioned by the
     storm,
Tossing to heaven my frontlet, wild and gray,
   Mateless, yet conscious ever of a warm
And brooding presence close to mine all day.

What is this alien thing, so near, so far,
   Close to my life always, but blending never?
Hemmed in by walls whose crystal gates unbar
   Not at the instance of my strong endeavor
To pierce the stronghold where their secrets are?

Buoyant, impalpable, relentless, thin,
   Rise the clear, mocking walls.   I strive in vain
To reach the pulsing heart that beats within,
   Or with persistence of a cold disdain,
To quell the gladness which I may not win.

Forever sundered and forever one,
    Linked by a bond whose spell I may not guess,
Our hostile, yet embracing currents run ;
    Such wedlock lonelier is than loneliness.
Baffled, withheld, I clasp the bride I shun.

Yet even in my wrath a wild regret
    Mingles ; a bitterness of jealous strife
Tinges my fury as I foam and fret
    Against the borders of that calmer life,
Beside whose course my wrathful course is set.

But all my anger, all my pain and woe,
    Are vain to daunt her gladness ; all the while
She goes rejoicing, and I do not know,
    Catching the soft irradiance of her smile,
If I am most her lover or her foe.

MY WHITE CHRYSANTHEMUM.

AS purely white as is the drifted snow,
　　More dazzling fair than summer roses are,
　　Petalled with rays like a clear rounded star,
When winds pipe chilly, and red sunsets glow,
　　Your blossoms blow.

Sweet with a freshening fragrance, all their own,
　　In which a faint, dim breath of bitter lies,
　　Like wholesome truth mid honeyed flatteries ;
When other blooms are dead, and birds have flown,
　　You stand alone.

Fronting the winter with a fearless grace,
　　Flavoring the odorless gray autumn chill,
　　Nipped by the furtive frosts, but cheery still,
Lifting to heaven from the bare garden place
　　A smiling face.

Roses are fair, but frail, and soon grow faint,
    Nor can endure a hardness; violets blue,
    Short-lived and sweet, live but a day or two;
The nun-like lily bows without complaint,
        And dies a saint.

Each following each they hasten them away,
    And leave us to our winter and our rue,
    Sad and uncomforted; you, only you,
Dear, hardy lover, keep your faith and stay
        Long as you may.

And so we choose you out from all the rest,
    For that most noble word of "Loyalty,"
    Which blazoned on your petals seems to be;
Winter is near, — stay with us; be our guest,
        The last and best.

TILL THE DAY DAWN.

WHY should I weary you, dear heart, with words,
   Words all discordant with a foolish pain?
   Thoughts cannot interrupt or prayers do wrong,
And soft and silent as the summer rain
Mine fall upon your pathway all day long.

Giving as God gives, counting not the cost
   Of broken box or spilled and fragrant oil,
I know that, spite of your strong carelessness,
   Rest must be sweeter, worthier must be toil,
Touched with such mute, invisible caress.

One of these days, our weary ways quite trod,
   Made free at last and unafraid of men,
I shall draw near and reach to you my hand.
   And you? Ah ! well, we shall be spirits then.
I think you will be glad and understand.

MY BIRTHDAY.

WHO is this who gently slips
    Through my door, and stands and sighs,
Hovering in a soft eclipse,
With a finger on her lips
    And a meaning in her eyes?

Once she came to visit me
    In white robes with festal airs,
Glad surprises, songs of glee ;
Now in silence cometh she,
    And a sombre garb she wears.

Once I waited and was tired,
    Chid her visits as too few ;
Crownless now and undesired,
She to seek me is inspired
    Oftener than she used to do.

Grave her coming is and still,
  Sober her appealing mien,
Tender thoughts her glances fill;
But I shudder, as one will
  When an open grave is seen.

Wherefore, friend, — for friend thou art, —
  Should I wrong thee thus and grieve?
Wherefore push thee from my heart?
Of my morning thou wert part;
  Be a part too of my eve.

See, I hold my hand to meet
  That cool, shadowy hand of thine;
Hold it firmly, it is sweet
Thus to clasp and thus to greet,
  Though no more in full sunshine.

Come and freely seek my door,
  I will open willingly;
I will chide the past no more,
Looking to the things before,
  Led by pathways known to thee.

BY THE CRADLE.

THE baby Summer lies asleep and dreaming —
   Dreaming and blooming like a guarded rose ;
And March, a kindly nurse, though rude of
    seeming,
   Is watching by the cradle hung with snows.

Her blowing winds but keep the rockers swinging,
   And deepen slumber in the shut blue eyes,
And the shrill cadences of her high singing
   Are to the babe but wonted lullabies.

She draws the coverlet white and tucks it trimly,
   She folds the little sleeper safe from harm,
Or bends to lift the veil, and, peering inly,
   Makes sure it lies all undisturbed and warm.

And so she sits, till in the still, gray dawning
   Two fairer nurses come, her place to take,
And smiling, beaming, with no word of warning,
   Draw off the quilt, and kiss the babe awake.

A THUNDER STORM.

THE day was hot and the day was dumb,
  Save for cricket's chirr or the bee's low hum,
    Not a bird was seen or a butterfly,
And ever till noon was over, the sun
  Glared down with a yellow and terrible eye;

Glared down in the woods, where the breathless boughs
Hung heavy and faint in a languid drowse,
  And the ferns were curling with thirst and heat;
Glared down on the fields where the sleepy cows
  Stood munching the grasses, dry and sweet.

Then a single cloud rose up in the west,
With a base of gray and a white, white crest;
  It rose and it spread a mighty wing,
And swooped at the sun, though he did his best
  And struggled and fought like a wounded thing.

8

And the woods awoke, and the sleepers heard,
Each heavily hanging leaflet stirred
   With a little expectant quiver and thrill,
As the cloud bent over and uttered a word, —
   One volleying, rolling syllable.

And once and again came the deep, low tone
Which only to thunder's lips is known,
   And the earth held up her fearless face
And listened as if to a signal blown, —
   A signal-trump in some heavenly place.

The trumpet of God, obeyed on high,
His signal to open the granary
   And send forth his heavily loaded wains
Rumbling and roaring down the sky
   And scattering the blessed, long-harvested rains.

THROUGH THE DOOR.

THE angel opened the door
    A little way,
And she vanished, as melts a star,
    Into the day.
And, for just a second's space,
    Ere the bar he drew,
The pitying angel paused,
    And we looked through.

What did we see within?
    Ah ! who can tell?
What glory and glow of light
    Ineffable ;
What peace in the very air,
    What hush and calm,
Soothing each tired soul
    Like healing balm !

Was it a dream we dreamed,
 Or did we hear
The harping of silver harps,
 Divinely clear?
A murmur of that "new song,"
 Which, soft and low,
The happy angels sing, —
 Sing as they go?

And, as in the legend old,
 The good monk heard,
As he paced his cloister dim,
 A heavenly bird,
And, rapt and lost in the joy
 Of the wondrous song,
Listened a hundred years,
 Nor deemed them long,

So chained in sense and limb,
 All blind with sun,
We stood and tasted the joy
 Of our vanished one;

And we took no note of time,
 Till soon or late
The gentle angel sighed,
 And shut the gate.

The vision is closed and sealed.
 We are come back
To the old, accustomed earth,
 The well-worn track, —
Back to the daily toil,
 The daily pain, —
But we never can be the same,
 Never again.

We who have bathed in noon,
 All radiant white,
Shall we come back content
 To sit in night?
Content with self and sin,
 The stain, the blot?
To have stood so near the gate
 And enter not?

O glimpse so swift, so sweet,
    So soon withdrawn !
Stay with us ; light our dusks
    Till day shall dawn ;
Until the shadows flee,
    And to our view
Again the gate unbars,
    And we pass through.

READJUSTMENT.

FTER the earthquake shock or lightning dart
Comes a recoil of silence o'er the lands,
And then, with pulses hot and quivering hands,
Earth calls up courage to her mighty heart,
Plies every tender, compensating art,
Draws her green, flowery veil above the scar,
Fills the shrunk hollow, smooths the riven plain,
And with a century's tendance heals again
The seams and gashes which her fairness mar.
So we, when sudden woe like lightning sped,
Finds us and smites us in our guarded place,
After one brief, bewildered moment's space,
By the same heavenly instinct taught and led,
Adjust our lives to loss, make friends with pain,
Bind all our shattered hopes and bid them bloom again.

AT THE GATE.

"For behold, the kingdom of God is within you."

HY kingdom here?
       Lord, can it be?
  Searching and seeking everywhere
       For many a year,
"Thy kingdom come" has been my prayer.
Was that dear kingdom all the while so near?

       Blinded and dull
       With selfish sin,
Have I been sitting at the gates
       Called Beautiful,
Where Thy fair angel stands and waits,
With hand upon the lock to let me in?

       Was I the wall
       Which barred the way,
Darkening the glory of Thy grace,
       Hiding the ray
Which, shining out as from Thy very face,
Had shown to other men the perfect day?

Was I the bar
Which shut me out
From the full joyance which they taste
Whose spirits are
Within Thy Paradise embraced, —
Thy blessed Paradise, which seemed so far?

The vision swells :
I seem to catch
Celestial breezes, rustling low,
The asphodels,
Where, singing softly ever to and fro,
Moves each fair saint who in Thy presence dwells.

Let me not sit
Another hour,
Idly awaiting what is mine to win,
Blinded in wit.
Lord Jesus, rend these walls of self and sin ;
Beat down the gate, that I may enter it.

A HOME.

HAT is a home?   A guarded space,
  Wherein a few, unfairly blest,
Shall sit together, face to face,
  And bask and purr and be at rest?

Where cushioned walls rise up between
  Its inmates and the common air,
The common pain, and pad and screen
  From blows of fate or winds of care?

Where Art may blossom strong and free,
  And Pleasure furl her silken wing,
And every laden moment be
  A precious and peculiar thing?

And Past and Future, softly veiled
  In hiding mists, shall float and lie
Forgotten half, and unassailed
  By either hope or memory,

While the luxurious Present weaves
　Her perfumed spells untried, untrue,
Broiders her garments, heaps her sheaves,
　All for the pleasure of a few?

Can it be this, the longed-for thing
　Which wanderers on the restless foam,
Unsheltered beggars, birds on wing,
　Aspire to, dream of, christen " Home"?

No.　Art may bloom, and peace and bliss;
　Grief may refrain and Death forget;
But if there be no more than this,
　The soul of home is wanting yet.

Dim image from far glory caught,
　Fair type of fairer things to be,
The true home rises in our thought,
　A beacon set for men to see.

Its lamps burn freely in the night,
　Its fire-glows unchidden shed
Their cheering and abounding light
　On homeless folk uncomforted.

Each sweet and secret thing within
  Gives out a fragrance on the air, —
A thankful breath, sent forth to win
  A little smile from others' care.

The few, they bask in closer heat;
  The many catch the further ray.
Life higher seems, the world more sweet,
  And hope and Heaven less far away.

So the old miracle anew
  Is wrought on earth and provéd good,
And crumbs apportioned for a few,
  God-blessed, suffice a multitude.

THE LEGEND OF KINTU.

WHEN earth was young and men were few,
And all things freshly born and new
Seemed made for blessing, not for ban,
Kintu, the god, appeared as man.
Clad in the plain white priestly dress,
He journeyed through the wilderness,
His wife beside.   A mild-faced cow
They drove, and one low-bleating lamb ;
He bore a ripe banana-bough,
And she a root of fruitful yam :
This was their worldly worth and store,
But God can make the little more.
The glad earth knew his feet ; her mould
Trembled with quickening thrills, and stirred.
Miraculous harvests spread and rolled,
The orchards shone with ruddy gold ;
The flocks increased, increased the herd,
And a great nation spread and grew
From the swift lineage of the two,

Peopling the solitary place ;
A fair and strong and fruitful race,
Who knew not pain nor want nor grief,
And Kintu reigned their lord and chief.

So sped three centuries along,
Till Kintu's sons waxed fierce and strong ;
They learned to war, they loved to slay ;
Cruel and dark grew all their faces ;
Discordant death-cries scared the day,
Blood stained the green and holy places ;
And drunk with lust, with anger hot,
His sons mild Kintu heeded not.
At last the god arose in wrath,
His sandals tied, and down the path,
His wife beside him, as of yore,
He went.   A cow, a single lamb
They took ; one tuber of the yam ;
One yellow-podded branch they bore
Of ripe banana, — these, no more,
Of all the heaped-up harvest store.
They left the huts, they left the tent,
Nor turned, nor cast a backward look :
Behind, the thick boughs met and shook.

They vanished.   Long with wild lament
Mourned all the tribe, in vain, in vain ;
The gift once given was given no more,
The grievéd god came not again.

To what far paradise they fared,
That heavenly pair, what wilderness
Their gentle rule next owned and shared,
Knoweth no man, — no man can guess.
On secret roads, by pathways blind,
The gods go forth, and none may find ;
But sad the world where God is not !
By man was Kintu soon forgot,
Or named and held as legend dim ;
But the wronged earth, remembering him,
By scanty fruit and tardy grain
And silent song revealed her pain.
So centuries came, and centuries went,
And heaped the graves and filled the tent.
Kings rose, and fought their royal way
To conquest over heaps of slain,
And reigned a little.   Then, one day,
They vanished into dust again,
And other kings usurped their place,

Who called themselves of Kintu's race,
And worshipped Kintu ; not as he,
The mild, benignant deity,
Who held all life a holy thing,
Be it of insect or of king,
Would have ordained, but with wild rite,
With altars heaped, and dolorous cries,
And savage dance, and bale-fires light,
An unaccepted sacrifice.
At last, when thousand years were flown,
The great Ma-anda filled the throne :
A prince of generous heart and high,
Impetuous, noble, fierce, and true ;
His wrath like lightning hurtling by,
His pardon like the healing dew.
And chiefs and sages swore each one
He was great Kintu's worthiest son.

One night, in forests still and deep,
A shepherd sat to watch his sheep,
And started, as through darkness dim
A strange voice rang and called to him :
"Wake ! there are wonders waiting thee !
Go where the thick mimosas be,

Fringing a little open plain.
Honor and power wouldest thou gain?
Go, foolish man, to fortune blind ;
Follow the stream, and thou shalt find."
Three several nights the voice was heard,
Louder and more emphatic grown.
Then, at the thrice-repeated word,
The shepherd rose and went alone,
Threading the mazes of the stream
Like one who wanders in a dream.
Long miles he ran, the stream beside,
Which this way, that way, turned and sped,
And called and sang, a noisy guide.
At last its vagrant dances led
To where the thick mimosas' shade
Circled and fringed an open glade ;
There the wild streamlet danced away,
The moon was shining strangely white,
And by its fitful, gleaming ray
The shepherd saw a wondrous sight ;
In the glade's midst, each on his mat,
A group of arméd warriors sat,
White-robed, majestic, with deep eyes
Fixed on him with a stern surprise ;

9

And in their midst an aged chief
Enthronéd sat, whose beard, like foam,
Caressed his mighty knees.   As leaf
Shakes in the wind the shepherd shook,
And veiled his eyes before that look,
And prayed, and thought upon his home,
Nor spoke, nor moved, till the old man,
In voice like waterfall, began :
" Shepherd, how names himself thy king? "
" Ma-anda," answered, shuddering,
The shepherd.   " Good, thou speakest well.
And now, my son, I bid thee tell
Thy first king's name."   " It was Kintu."
" 'T is rightly said, thou answerest true.
Hark !   To Ma-anda, Kintu's son,
Hasten, and bid him, fearing naught,
Come hither, taking thee for guide ;
Thou and he, not another one,
Not even a dog may run beside !
Long has Ma-anda Kintu sought
With spell and conjuration dim,
Now Kintu has a word for him.
Go, do thy errand, haste thee hence,
Kintu insures thy recompense."

All night the shepherd ran, star-led,
All the hot day he hastened straight,
Nor stopped for sleep, nor stopped for bread,
Until he reached the city gate,
And saw red rays of evening fall
On the leaf-hutted capital.
He sought the king, his tale he told.
Ma-anda faltered not, nor stayed.
He seized his spear, he left the tent;
Shook off the brown arms of his queens,
Who clasped his knees with wailing screams;
On pain of instant death forbade
That man should spy or follow him;
And down the pathway, arching dim,
Fearless and light of heart and bold
Followed the shepherd where he went.

But one there was who loved his king
Too well to suffer such strange thing, —
The chieftain of the host was he,
Next to the monarch in degree;
And, fearing wile or stratagem
Menaced the king, he followed them
With noiseless tread and out of sight.

So on they fared the forest through,
From evening shades to dawning light,
From dawning to the dusk and dew, —
The unseen follower and the two.
Ofttimes the king turned back to scan,
The path, but never saw he man.
At last the forest-guarded space
They reached, where, ranged in order, sat,
Each couched upon his braided mat,
The white-robed warriors, face to face
With their majestic chief.   The king,
Albeit unused to fear or awe,
Bowed down in homage, wondering,
And bent his eyes, as fearing to be
Blinded by rays of deity.
Then asked the mighty voice and calm,
" Art thou Ma-anda called?"   " I am."
" And art thou king?"   " The king am I,"
The bold Ma-anda made reply.
" 'T is rightly spoken ; but, my son,
Why hast thou my command forgot,
That no man with thee to this spot
Should come, except thy guide alone?"
" No man has come," Ma-anda said.

"Alone we journeyed, he and I ;
And often have I turned my head,
And never living thing could spy.
None is there, on my faith as king."
" A king's word is a weighty thing,"
The old man answered. " Let it be, —
But still a man *has* followed thee !
Now answer, Ma-anda, one more thing :
Who, first of all thy line, was king?"
" Kintu the god." " 'T is well, my son,
All creatures Kintu loved, — not one
Too pitiful or weak or small ;
He knew them and he loved them all ;
And never did a living thing,
Or bird in air or fish in lake,
Endure a pang for Kintu's sake.
Then rose his sons, of differing mind,
Who gorged on cruel feasts each day,
And bathed in blood, and joyed to slay,
And laughed at pain and suffering.
Then Kintu sadly went his way.
The gods long-suffering are and kind,
Often they pardon, long they wait ;
But men are evil, men are blind.

After much tarriance, much debate,
The good gods leave them to their fate ;
So Kintu went where none may find.

Each king in turn has sought since then,
From Chora down, the first in line,
To win lost Kintu back to men.
Vain was his search, and vain were thine,
Save that the gods have special grace
To thee, Ma-anda.   Face to face
With Kintu thou shalt stand, and he
Shall speak the word of power to thee ;
Clasped to his bosom, thou shalt share
His knowledge of the earth, the air,
And deep things, secret things, shalt learn.
But stay," — the old man's voice grew stern, —
" Before I further speak, declare
Who is that man in ambush there ! "
" There is no man, — no man I see."
" Deny no longer, it is vain.
Within the shadow of the tree
He lurketh ; lo, behold him plain ! "
And the king saw ; — for at the word
From covert stole the hidden spy,

And sought his monarch's side. One cry,
A lion's roar, Ma-anda gave,
Then seized his spear, and poised and drave.
Like lightning bolt it hissed and whirred,
A flash across the midnight blue.
A single groan, a jet of red,
And, pierced and stricken through and through,
Upon the ground the chief fell dead ;
But still with love no death could chase,
His eyes sought out his master's face.

Blent with Ma-anda's a wild cry
Of many voices rose on high,
A shriek of anguish and despair,
Which shook and filled the startled air ;
And when the king, his wrath still hot,
Turned him, the little grassy plain
All lonely in the moonlight lay :
The chiefs had vanished all away
As melted into thin, blue wind ;
Gone was the old man. Stunned and blind,
For a long moment stood the king ;
He tried to wake ; he rubbed his eyes,
As though some fearful dream to end.

It was no dream, this fearful thing :
There was the forest, there the skies,
The shepherd — and his murdered friend.
With feverish haste, bewildered, mazed,
This way and that he vainly sped,
Beating the air like one half crazed ;
With prayers and cries unnumberéd,
Searching, imploring, — vain, all vain.
Only the echoing woods replied,
With mocking booms their long aisles through,
" Come back, Kintu, Kintu, Kintu ! "
And pitiless to all his pain
The unanswering gods his suit denied.
At last, as dawning slowly crept
To day, the king sank down and wept
A space ; then, lifting as they could
The lifeless burden, once a man,
He and the shepherd-guide began
Their grievous journey through the wood,
The long and hard and dreary way,
Trodden so lightly yesterday ;
And the third day, at evening's fall,
Gained the leaf-hutted capital.
There burial rites were duly paid :

Like bridegroom decked for banqueting,
The chief adorned his funeral-pyre ;
Rare gums and spices fed the fire,
Perfumes and every precious thing ;
And songs were sung, and prayers were prayed,
And priests danced jubilant all day.
But prone the king Ma-anda lay,
With ashes on his royal crest,
And groaned, and beat upon his breast,
And called on Kintu loud and wild :
" Father, come back, forgive thy child ! "
Bitter the cry, but vain, all vain ;
The grievéd god came not again.

EASTER.

HEN dawns on earth the Easter sun
  The dear saints feel an answering thrill.
  With whitest flowers their hands they fill ;
And, singing all in unison,

Unto the battlements they press —
  The very marge of heaven — how near !
  And bend, and look upon us here
With eyes that rain down tenderness.

Their roses, brimmed with fragrant dew,
  Their lilies fair they raise on high ;
  "Rejoice ! The Lord is risen !" they cry ;
"Christ is arisen ; we prove it true !

" Rejoice, and dry those faithless tears
  With which your Easter flowers are stained ;
  Share in our bliss, who have attained
The rapture of the eternal years ;

" Have proved the promise which endures,
　　The Love that deigned, the Love that died ;
　　Have reached our haven by His side —
Are Christ's, but none the less are yours ;

" Yours with a nearness never known
　　While parted by the veils of sense ;
　　Infinite knowledge, joy intense,
A love which is not love alone,

" But faith perfected, vision free,
　　And patience limitless and wise —
　　Beloved, the Lord is risen, arise !
And dare to be as glad as we ! "

We do rejoice, we do give thanks,
　　O blessed ones, for all your gain,
　　As dimly through these mists of pain
We catch the gleaming of your ranks.

We will arise, with zeal increased,
　　Blending, the while we strive and grope,
　　Our paler festival of Hope
With your Fruition's perfect feast.

Bend low, beloved ; against the blue,
  Lift higher still the lilies fair,
  Till, following where our treasures are,
We come to join the feast with you.

BIND-WEED.

IN the deep shadow of the porch
 A slender bind-weed springs,
And climbs, like airy acrobat,
 The trellises, and swings
And dances in the golden sun
 In fairy loops and rings.

Its cup-shaped blossoms, brimmed with dew,
 Like pearly chalices,
Hold cooling fountains, to refresh
 The butterflies and bees ;
And humming-birds on vibrant wings
 Hover, to drink at ease.

And up and down the garden-beds,
 Mid box and thyme and yew,
And spikes of purple lavender,
 And spikes of larkspur blue,
The bind-weed tendrils win their way,
 And find a passage through.

With touches coaxing, delicate,
  And arts that never tire,
They tie the rose-trees each to each,
  The lilac to the brier,
Making for graceless things a grace,
  With steady, sweet desire.

Till near and far the garden growths,
  The sweet, the frail, the rude,
Draw close, as if with one consent,
  And find each other good,
Held by the bind-weed's pliant loops,
  In a dear brotherhood.

Like one fair sister, slender, arch,
  A flower in bloom and poise,
Gentle and merry and beloved,
  Making no stir or noise,
But swaying, linking, blessing all
  A family of boys.

APRIL.

ARK ! upon the east-wind, piping, creeping,
   Comes a voice all clamorous with despair ;
  It is April, crying sore and weeping,
O'er the chilly earth, so brown and bare.

"When I went away," she murmurs, sobbing,
  " All my violet-banks were starred with blue ;
Who, O, who has been here, basely robbing
  Bloom and odor from the fragrant crew ?

" Who has reft the robin's hidden treasure, —
  All the speckled spheres he loved so well ?
And the buds which danced in merry measure
  To the chiming of the hyacinth's bell ?

" Where are all my hedge-rows, flushed with Maying ?
  And the leafy rain, that tossed so fair,
Like the spray from silver fountains playing,
  Where the elm-tree's column rose in air ?

" All are vanished, and my heart is breaking;
    And my tears they slowly drip and fall;
Only death could listen without waking
    To the grief and passion of my call ! "

Thus she plaineth.   Then ten million voices,
    Tiny, murmurous, like drops of rain,
Raised in song as when the wind rejoices,
    Ring the answer, " We are here again.

" We were hiding, April.   Did you miss us?
    None of us were really gone away;
Stoop thy pretty head and gently kiss us
    Once before we all come out to play.

" Here are all the clustering buds of roses,
    And the dandelion's mimic sun;
Of thy much-beloved and vanished posies
    None are missing, not a single one ! "

Little points of green push out to greet her,
    Little creepers grasp her garment's hem,
Hidden sweetnesses grow ever sweeter
    As she bends and brightly smiles at them.

Every tear is answered by a blossom,
   Every sigh with songs and laughter blent,
Apple-blooms upon the breezes toss them.
   April knows her own. and is content.

MAY.

EW flowery scents strewed everywhere,
New sunshine poured in largesse fair,
   " We shall be happy now," we say.
A voice just trembles through the air,
   And whispers, " May."

Nay, but we *must!*   No tiny bud
But thrills with rapture at the flood
   Of fresh young life which stirs to-day.
The same wild thrill irradiates our blood ;
   Why hint of " May "?

For us are coming fast and soon
The delicate witcheries of June ;
   July, with ankles deep in hay ;
The bounteous Autumn.   Like a mocking tune
   Again sounds, " May."

Spring's last-born darling, clear-eyed, sweet,
Pauses a moment, with white twinkling feet,
   And golden locks in breezy play,
Half teasing and half tender, to repeat
     Her song of " May."

Ah, month of hope ! all promised glee,
All merry meanings, lie in thee ;
   Surely no cloud can daunt thy day.
The ripe lips part in smiling mockery,
     And murmur, " May."

Still from the smile a comfort may we glean ;
Although our " must-be's," " shall-be's," idle seem,
   Close to our hearts one little word we lay :
We may not be as happy as we dream,
     But then we — may.

SECRETS.

IN the long, bright summer, dear to bird and bee,
   When the woods are standing in liveries green
         and gay,
Merry little voices sound from every tree,
   And they whisper secrets all the day.

If we knew the language, we should hear strange things;
   Mrs. Chirry, Mrs. Flurry, deep in private chat.
"How are all your nestlings, dear? Do they use their
      wings?
What was that sad tale about a cat?"

"Where is your new cottage?" "Hush! I pray you,
      hush!
Please speak very softly, dear, and make no noise.
It is on the lowest bough of the lilac bush,
   And I am so dreadfully afraid of boys.

" Mr. Chirry chose the spot, without consulting me ;
   Such a very public place, and insecure for it.
I can scarcely sleep at night for nervousness ; but he
   Says I am a silly thing and does n't mind a bit."

" So the Bluebirds have contracted, have they, for a house ?
   And a nest is under way for little Mr. Wren ?
Hush, dear, hush ! Be quiet, dear ; quiet as a mouse.
   These are weighty secrets, and we must whisper them."

Close the downy dowagers nestle on the bough
   While the timorous voices soften low with dread,
And we, walking underneath, little reckon how
   Mysteries are couching in the tree-tops overhead.

Ah, the pretty whisperers ! It was very well
   When the leaves were thick and green, awhile ago —
Leaves are secret-keepers ; but since the last leaf fell
   There is nothing hidden from the eyes below.

Bared are the brown tenements, and all the world may see
   What Mrs. Chirry, Mrs. Flurry, hid so close that day.
In the place of rustling wings, cold winds rustling be,
   And thickly lie the icicles where once the warm brood lay.

Shall we tease the birdies, when they come back in spring, —
    Tease and tell them we have fathomed all their secrets
       small,
Every secret hiding-place and dear and precious thing,
    Which they left behind the leaves, the red leaves, in the
       fall?

They would only laugh at us and wink their saucy eyes,
    And answer, " Last year's secrets are all past and told.
New years bring new happenings and fresh mysteries,
    You are very welcome to the stale ones of the old ! "

HOW THE LEAVES CAME DOWN.

'LL tell you how the leaves came down.
　　The great Tree to his children said,
　"You 're getting sleepy, Yellow and Brown,
　Yes, very sleepy, little Red ;
　It is quite time you went to bed."

"Ah !" begged each silly, pouting leaf,
　" Let us a little longer stay ;
Dear Father Tree, behold our grief,
　'T is such a very pleasant day
　We do not want to go away."

So, just for one more merry day
　To the great Tree the leaflets clung,
Frolicked and danced and had their way,
　Upon the autumn breezes swung,
　Whispering all their sports among,

"Perhaps the great Tree will forget
And let us stay until the spring,
If we all beg and coax and fret."
But the great Tree did no such thing;
He smiled to hear their whispering.

"Come, children all, to bed," he cried;
And ere the leaves could urge their prayer
He shook his head, and far and wide,
Fluttering and rustling everywhere,
Down sped the leaflets through the air.

I saw them; on the ground they lay,
Golden and red, a huddled swarm,
Waiting till one from far away,
White bed-clothes heaped upon her arm,
Should come to wrap them safe and warm.

The great bare Tree looked down and smiled.
"Good-night, dear little leaves," he said;
And from below each sleepy child
Replied "Good-night," and murmured,
"It is *so* nice to go to bed."

BARCAROLES.

I.

OVER the lapsing lagune all the day
    Urging my gondola with oar-strokes light,
  Always beside one shadowy waterway
I pause and peer, with eager, jealous sight,
Toward the Piazza where Pepita stands,
  Wooing the hungry pigeons from their flight.

Dark the canal; but she shines like the sun,
  With yellow hair and dreaming, wine-brown eyes.
Thick crowd the doves for food.   She gives *me* none.
  She sees and will not see.   Vain are my sighs.
One slow, reluctant stroke.   Aha ! she turns,
  Gestures and smiles, with coy and feigned surprise.

Shifting and baffling is our Lido track,
　　Blind and bewildering are the currents flow.
Me' they perplex not.　In the midnight black
　　I hold my way secure and fearless row.
But ah ! what chart have I to her, my Sea,
　　Whose fair, mysterious depths I long to know?

Subtle as sad mirage ; true and untrue
　　She seems, and, pressing ever on in vain,
I yearn across the mocking, tempting blue.
　　Never she draws more near, never I gain
A furlong's space toward where she sits and smiles ;
　　Smiles and cares nothing for my love and pain.

How shall I win her?　What may strong arm do
　　Against such gentle distance?　I can say
No more than this, that when she stands to woo
　　The doves beside the shadowy waterway,
And when I look and long, sometimes — she smiles !
　　Perhaps she will do more than smile one day l

II.

LIGHT and darkness, brown and fair,
  Ha ! they think I do not see, —
I behind them, swiftly rowing.
  Rowing? Yes, but eyes are free,
    Eyes and fancies : —

Now what fire in looks and glances !
  Now the dark head bends, grown bolder.
Ringlets mingle — silence — broken
  (All unconscious of beholder)
    By a kiss !

What could lovers ask or miss
  In such moonlight, such June weather,
But a boat like this, (me rowing !)
  And forever and together
    To be floating?

Ah ! if she and I such boating
  Might but share one day, some fellow
With strong arms behind, Pasquale,
  Or Luigi, with gay awning,
    (She likes yellow !)

She — I mean Pepita — mellow
　Moonlight on the waves, no other
To break silence or catch whispers,
　All the love which now I smother
　　Told and spoken, —

Listened to, a kiss for token :
　How, my Signor?　What ! so soon
Homeward bound?　We, born of Venice,
　Live by night and nap by noon.
　　If 't were me, now,

With *my* brown-eyed girl, this prow
　Would not turn for hours still ;
But the Signor bids, *commandi !*
　I am here to do his will,
　　He is master.

Glide we on ; so, faster, faster.
　Now the two are safely landed.
Buono mano, grazie, Signor,
　They who love are open-handed.
　　Now, Pepita !

III.

TORCELLO.

SHE has said " yes," and the world is a-smile.
  There she sits as she sat in my dream ;
  There she sits, and the blue waves gleam,
And the current bears us along the while
For happy mile after happy mile,
  A fairy boat on a fairy stream.

The Angelus bells swing to and fro,
  And the sunset lingers to hear their swell,
  For the sunset loves such music well.
A big, bright moon is hovering low,
Where the edge of the sky is all aglow,
  · Like the middle heart of a red, red shell.

The Lido floats like a purple flower ;
  Orange and rose are the sails at sea ;
  Silver and pink the surf-line free

·· Tumbles and chimes, and the perfect hour
Clasps us and folds us in its power,
  Folds us and holds us, my love and me.

Can there be sadness anywhere
    In the world to-night?   Or tears or sighs
    Beneath such festal moon and skies?
Can there be memory or despair?
What is it, beloved?   Why point you there,
    With sudden dew in those dearest eyes?

Yes ! one sad thing on the happy earth !
    Like a mourner's veil in the bridal array,
    Or a sorrowful sigh in the music gay,
A shade on the sun, in the feast a dearth,
    Drawn like a ghost across our way,
Torcello sits and rebukes our mirth.

She sits a widow who sat as queen,
    Ashes on brows once crowned and bright;
    Woe in the eyes once full of light;
Her sad, fair roses and manifold green,
    All bitter and pallid and heavy with night,
Are full of the shadows of woes unseen.

Let us hurry away from her face unblest,
  Row us away, for the song is done,
  The Angelus bells cease, one by one,
Pepita's head lies on my breast;
But, trembling and full of a vague unrest,
  I long for the morrow and for the sun.

MY RIGHTS.

YES, God has made me a woman,
    And I am content to be
  Just what He meant, not reaching out
For other things, since He
Who knows me best and loves me most has ordered this
      for me.

A woman, to live my life out
    In quiet womanly ways,
Hearing the far-off battle,
    Seeing as through a haze
The crowding, struggling world of men fight through their
      busy days.

I am not strong or valiant,
    I would not join the fight
Or jostle with crowds in the highways
    To sully my garments white ;
But I have rights as a woman, and here I claim my right.

The right of a rose to bloom
 In its own sweet, separate way,
With none to question the perfumed pink
 And none to utter a nay
If it reaches a root or points a thorn, as even a rose-tree
  may.

The right of the lady-birch to grow,
 To grow as the Lord shall please,
By never a sturdy oak rebuked,
 Denied nor sun nor breeze,
For all its pliant slenderness, kin to the stronger trees.

The right to a life of my own, —
 Not merely a casual bit
Of the life of somebody else, flung out
 That, taking hold of it,
I may stand as a cipher does after a numeral writ.

The right to gather and glean
 What food I need and can
From the garnered store of knowledge
 Which man has heaped for man,
Taking with free hands freely and after an ordered plan.

The right — ah, best and sweetest ! —
　　To stand all undismayed
Whenever sorrow or want or sin
　　Call for a woman's aid,
With none to cavil or question, by never a look gainsaid.

I do not ask for a ballot ;
　　Though very life were at stake,
I would beg for the nobler justice
　　That men for manhood's sake
Should give ungrudgingly, nor withhold till I must fight
　　and take.

The fleet foot and the feeble foot
　　Both seek the self-same goal,
The weakest soldier's name is writ
　　On the great army-roll,
And God, who made man's body strong, made too the
　　woman's soul.

SOLSTICE.

I.

I SIT at evening's scented close,
   In fulness of the summer-tide ;
All dewy fair the lily glows,
No single petal of the rose
   Has fallen to dim the rose's pride.

Sweet airs, sweet harmonies of hue,
   Surround, caress me everywhere ;
The spells of dusk, the spells of dew,
My senses steal, my reason woo,
   And sing a lullaby to care.

But vainly do the warm airs sing,
   All vain the roses' rapturous breath ;
A chill blast, as from wintry wing,
Smites on my heart, and, shuddering,
   I see the beauty changed to death.

Afar I see it loom and rise,
  That pitiless and icy shape.
It blots the blue, it dims the skies;
Amid the summer land it cries,
  " I come, and there is no escape !"

O, bitter drop in bloom and sweet !
  O, canker on the smiling day !
Have we but climbed the hill to meet
Thy fronting face, thy eyes of sleet?
  To hate, yet dare not turn away?

II.

I SIT beneath a leaden sky,
  Amid the piled and drifted snow;
My feet are on the graves where lie
The roses which made haste to die
  So long, so very long ago.

The sobbing wind is fierce and strong,
  Its cry is like a human wail,
But in my heart it sings this song:
" Not long, O Lord ! O Lord, not long !
  Surely thy spring-time shall prevail."

Out of the darkness and the cold,
   Out of the wintry depths I lean,
And lovingly I clasp and hold
The promises, and see unrolled
   A vision of the summer green.

O, life in death, sweet plucked from pain !
   O, distant vision fair to see !
Up the long hill we press and strain ;
We can bear all things and attain,
   If once our faces turn to Thee !

IN THE MIST.

SITTING all day in a silver mist,
  In silver silence all the day,
  Save for the low, soft hiss of spray,
And the lisp of sands by waters kissed,
  As the tide draws up the bay.

Little I hear and nothing I see,
  Wrapped in that veil by fairies spun ;
The solid earth is vanished for me,
And the shining hours speed noiselessly,
  A web of shadow and sun.

Suddenly out of the shifting veil
  A magical bark, by the sunbeams lit,
  Flits like a dream, — or seems to flit, —
With a golden prow and a gossamer sail,
  And the waves make room for it.

A fair, swift bark from some radiant realm,
  Its diamond cordage cuts the sky
  In glittering lines ; all silently
A seeming spirit holds the helm
  And steers : will he pass me by?

Ah, not for me is the vessel here !
  Noiseless and fast as a sea-bird's flight,
  She swerves and vanishes from my sight ;
No flap of sail, no parting cheer, —
  She has passed into the light.

Sitting some day in a deeper mist,
  Silent, alone, some other day,
  An unknown bark from an unknown bay,
By unknown waters lapped and kissed,
  Shall near me through the spray.

No flap of sail, no scraping of keel :
  Shadowy, dim, with a banner dark,
It will hover, will pause, and I shall feel
A hand which beckons, and, shivering, steal
  To the cold strand and embark.

Embark for that far mysterious realm,
   Whence the fathomless, trackless waters flow.
   Shall I see a Presence dim, and know
A Gracious Hand upon the helm,
   Nor be afraid to go?

And through black wave and stormy blast,
   And out of the fog-wreath dense and dun,
   Guided and held, shall the vessel run,
Gain the fair haven, night being past,
   And anchor in the sun?

WITHIN.

COULD my heart hold another one?
    I cannot tell.
Sometimes it seems an ample dome,
    Sometimes a cell.

Sometimes a temple filled with saints,
    Serene and fair,
Whose eyes are pure from mortal taints
    As lilies are.

Sometimes a narrow shrine, in which
    One precious face
Smiles ever from its guarded niche,
    With deathless grace.

Sometimes a nest, where weary things,
    And weak and shy,
Are brooded under mother wings
    Till they can fly.

And then a palace, with wide rooms
  Adorned and dressed,
Where eager slaves pour sweet perfumes
  For each new guest.

Whiche'er it be, I know always
  Within that door —
Whose latch it is not mine to raise —
  Blows evermore,

With breath of balm upon its wing,
  A soft, still air,
Which makes each closely folded thing
  Look always fair.

My darlings, do you feel me near,
  As every day
Into this hidden place and dear
  I take my way?

Always you stand in radiant guise,
  Always I see
A noiseless welcome in the eyes
  You turn on me.

And, whether I come soon or late,
    Whate'er befall,
Always within the guarded gate
    I find you all.

MENACE.

LL green and fair the Summer lies,
  Just budded from the bud of Spring,
With tender blue of wistful skies,
  And winds which softly sing.

Her clock has struck its morning hours ;
  Noon nears — the flowery dial is true ;
But still the hot sun veils its powers,
  In deference to the dew.

Yet there amid the fresh new green,
  Amid the young broods overhead,
A single scarlet branch is seen,
  Swung like a banner red ;

Tinged with the fatal hectic flush
  Which, when October frosts are near,
Flames on each dying tree and bush,
  To deck the dying year.

And now the sky seems not so blue,
  The yellow sunshine pales its ray,
A sorrowful, prophetic hue
  Lies on the radiant day,

As mid the bloom and tenderness
  I catch that scarlet menace there,
Like a gray sudden wintry tress
  Set in a child's bright hair.

The birds sing on, the roses blow,
  But like a discord heard but now.
A stain upon the petal's snow
  Is that one sad, red bough.

"HE THAT BELIEVETH SHALL NOT MAKE HASTE."

THE aloes grow upon the sand,
　　The aloes thirst with parching heat;
　　Year after year they waiting stand,
　Lonely and calm, and front the beat
　Of desert winds; and still a sweet
And subtle voice thrills all their veins:
" Great patience wins; it still remains,
After a century of pains,
　To you to bloom and be complete."

I grow upon a thorny waste;
　　Hot noontide lies on all the way,
And with its scorching breath makes haste
　　Each freshening dawn to burn and slay,
　　Yet patiently I bide and stay:
Knowing the secret of my fate,
The hour of bloom, dear Lord, I wait,
Come when it will, or soon or late,
　　A hundred years are but a day.

MY LITTLE GHOST.

KNOW where it lurks and hides,
　In the midst of the busy house,
　In the midst of the children's glee,
All day its shadow bides :
　Nobody knows but me.

On a closet-shelf it dwells,
　In the darkest corner of all,
　Mid rolls of woollen and fur,
And faint, forgotten smells
　Of last year's lavender.

That a ghost has its dwelling there
　Nobody else would guess, —
　"Only a baby's shoe,
A curl of golden hair,"
　You would say, "a toy or two, —

" A broken doll, whose lips
   And cheeks of waxen bloom
   Show dents of fingers small, —
Little, fair finger-tips, —
   A worn sash, — that is all."

Little to see or to guess ;
   But whenever I open the door,
   There, faithful to its post,
With its eyes' sad tenderness,
   I see my little ghost.

And I hasten to shut the door,
   I shut it tight and fast,
   Lest the sweet, sad thing get free,
Lest it flit beside on the floor,
   And sadden the day for me,

Lest between me and the sun,
   And between me and the heavens,
   And the laugh in the children's eyes,
The shadowy feet should run,
   The faint gold curls arise

Like a gleam of moonlight pale,
   And all the warmth and the light
   Should die from the summer day,
And the laughter turn to wail,
   And I should forget to pray.

So I keep the door shut fast,
   And my little ghost shut in,
   And whenever I cross the hall
I shiver and hurry past ;
   But I love it best of all.

CHRISTMAS.

OW did they keep his birthday then,
  The little fair Christ, so long ago?
O, many there were to be housed and fed,
And there was no place in the inn, they said,
  So into the manger the Christ must go,
To lodge with the cattle and not with men.

The ox and the ass they munched their hay,
  They munched and they slumbered, wondering not,
And out in the midnight cold and blue
The shepherds slept, and the sheep slept too,
  Till the angels' song and the bright star ray
Guided the wise men to the spot.

But only the wise men knelt and praised,
  And only the shepherds came to see,
And the rest of the world cared not at all
For the little Christ in the oxen's stall;
  And we are angry and amazed
That such a dull, hard thing should be !

How do we keep his birthday now?
  We ring the bells and we raise the strain,
We hang up garlands everywhere
And bid the tapers twinkle fair,
  . And feast and frolic — and then we go
Back to the same old lives again.

Are we so better, then, than they
  Who failed the new-born Christ to see?
To them a helpless babe, — to us
He shines a Saviour glorious,
  Our Lord, our Friend, our All — yet we
Are half asleep this Christmas day.

BENEDICAM DOMINO.

THANK God for life : life is not sweet always.
   Hands may be heavy-laden, hearts care full,
Unwelcome nights follow unwelcome days,
And dreams divine end in awakenings dull.
Still it is life, and life is cause for praise.
This ache, this restlessness, this quickening sting,
Prove me no torpid and inanimate thing,
Prove me of Him who is of life the Spring.
I am alive ! — and that is beautiful.

Thank God for Love : though Love may hurt and woun
Though set with sharpest thorns its rose may be,
Roses are not of winter, all attuned
Must be the earth, full of soft stir, and free
And warm ere dawns the rose upon its tree.
Fresh currents through my frozen pulses run ;
My heart has tasted summer, tasted sun,
And I can thank Thee, Lord, although not one
Of all the many roses blooms for me.

Thank God for Death : bright thing with dreary name,
We wrong with mournful flowers her pure, still brow.
We heap her with reproaches and with blame,
Her goodness and her fitness disallowed,
Questioning bitterly her why and how.
But calmly mid the clamor and surmise
She touches each in turn, and each grows wise.
Taught by the light in her mysterious eyes,
I *shall* be glad, and I am thankful now.

University Press: John Wilson & Son, Cambridge.

A FEW MORE VERSES.

By SUSAN COOLIDGE.

A

FEW MORE VERSES.

By SUSAN COOLIDGE, ꝑᴬᴰᴸⁱ

AUTHOR OF "VERSES."

BOSTON:

ROBERTS BROTHERS.

1891.

𝔘𝔫𝔦𝔟𝔢𝔯𝔰𝔦𝔱𝔶 𝔓𝔯𝔢𝔰𝔰:
JOHN WILSON AND SON, CAMBRIDGE.

GIVING to all, thou gavest as well to me.
    A myriad thirsty shores await the tide:
They drink and drink, and will not be denied;
But not a drop less full the brimming Sea.

One tiny shell among the kelp and weed,
One sand-grain where the beaches stretch away, —
How shall the tide regard them ?   Yet each day
It comes, and fills and satisfies their need.

What can the singing sands give to the Sea ?
What the dumb shell, though inly it rejoice ?
Only the echo of its own strong voice ; —
And this is all that here I bring to thee.

A BENEDICTION.

GOD give thee, love, thy heart's desire!
  What better can I pray?
For though love falter not, nor tire,
  And stand on guard all day,
How little can it know or do,
  How little can it say!

How hard it strives, and how in vain,
  By hope and fear misled,
To make the pathway soft and plain
  For the dear feet to tread,
To shield from sun-beat and from rain
  The one beloved head!

Its wisdom is made foolishness;
  Its best intent goes wrong;
It curses where it fain would bless,
  Is weak instead of strong, —
Marring with sad, discordant sighs
  The joyance of its song.

I do not dare to bless or ban, —
  I am too blind to see, —
But this one little prayer I can
  Put up to God for thee,
Because I know what fair, pure things
  Thy inmost wishes be;

That what thy heart desires the most
 Is what he loves to grant, —
The love that counteth not its cost
 If any crave or want ;
The presence of the Holy Ghost,
 The soul's inhabitant ;

The wider vision of the mind ;
 The spirit bright with sun ;
The temper like a fragrant wind,
 Chilling and grieving none ;
The quickened heart to know God's will
 And on his errands run ;

The ministry of little things, —
 Not counted mean or small
By that dear alchemy which brings
 Some grain of gold from all ;
The faith to wait as well as work,
 Whatever may befall.

So, sure of thee, and unafraid,
 I make my daily prayer,
Nor fear that my blind zeal be made
 Thy injury or snare :
God give thee, love, thy heart's desire,
 And bless thee everywhere !

CONTENTS.

CONTENTS.

xii   *CONTENTS.*

TO ARCITE AT THE WARS.

1759.

A THOUSAND leagues of wind-blown space,
  A thousand leagues of sea,
Half of the great earth's hiding face
  Divides mine eyes from thee ;
The world is strong, the waves are wide,
  But my good-will is stronger still,
My love, than wind or tide.

These sentinels which Fate has set
  To bar and hold me here
I make my errand-men, to get
  A message to thine ear.
The winds shall waft, the waters bear,
  And spite of seas I, when I please,
Can reach thee everywhere.

Prayers are like birds to find the way ;
  Thoughts have a swifter flight ;
And mine stream forth to thee all day,
  Nor stop to rest by night.

Like silent angels at thy side
    They stand unseen, they bend and lean,
They bless and warn and guide.

There is no near, there is no far,
    There is no loss or change,
To love which, like a fixèd star,
    Abideth in one range,
And shines, and shines, with quenchless eyes,
    And sends long rays in many ways
To lighten distant skies.

Where sight is not, faith brighter burns ;
    So faithfully I wait,
Secure that loyal loving earns
    Its guerdon soon or late, —
Secure, though lacking word or sign,
    That thy true thought keeps as it ought
Tryst with each thought of mine.

NEW EVERY MORNING.

VERY day is a fresh beginning,
  Every morn is the world made new.
You who are weary of sorrow and sinning,
  Here is a beautiful hope for you, —
  A hope for me and a hope for you.

All the past things are past and over ;
  The tasks are done and the tears are shed.
Yesterday's errors let yesterday cover ;
  Yesterday's wounds, which smarted and bled,
  Are healed with the healing which night has shed.

Yesterday now is a part of forever,
  Bound up in a sheaf, which God holds tight,
With glad days, and sad days, and bad days, which never
  Shall visit us more with their bloom and their blight,
  Their fulness of sunshine or sorrowful night.

Let them go, since we cannot re-live them,
  Cannot undo and cannot atone ;

God in his mercy receive, forgive them !
    Only the new days are our own ;
    To-day is ours, and to-day alone.

Here are the skies all burnished brightly,
    Here is the spent earth all re-born,
Here are the tired limbs springing lightly
    To face the sun and to share with the morn
    In the chrism of dew and the cool of dawn.

Every day is a fresh beginning ;
    Listen, my soul, to the glad refrain,
And, spite of old sorrow and older sinning,
    And puzzles forecasted and possible pain,
    Take heart with the day, and begin again.

LOHENGRIN.

TO have touched Heaven and failed to enter in !
Ah, Elsa, prone upon the lonely shore,
 Watching the swan-wings beat along the blue,
Watching the glimmer of the silver mail,
 Like flash of foam, till all are lost to view, —
What may thy sorrow or thy watch avail?
  He cometh nevermore.

All gone the new hope of thy yesterday, —
The tender gaze and strong, like dewy fire,
 The gracious form with airs of Heaven bedight,
The love that warmed thy being like a sun : —
 Thou hadst thy choice of noonday or of night ;
Now the swart shadows gather, one by one,
  To give thee thy desire !

To every life one heavenly chance befalls ;
To every soul a moment, big with fate,
 When, grown importunate with need and fear,

It cries for help, and lo ! from close at hand,
   The voice Celestial answers, " I am here ! "
Oh, blessed souls, made wise to understand,
   Made bravely glad to wait !

But thou, pale watcher on the lonely shore,
Where the surf thunders, and the foam-bells fly,
   Is there no place for penitence and pain,
No saving grace in thy all-piteous rue ?
   Will the bright vision never come again ?
Alas, the swan-wings vanish in the blue,
   There cometh no reply !

A SINGLE STITCH.

ONE stitch dropped as the weaver drove
 His nimble shuttle to and fro,
 In and out, beneath, above,
Till the pattern seemed to bud and grow
As if the fairies had helping been, —
One small stitch which could scarce be seen.
But the one stitch dropped pulled the next stitch out,
And a weak place grew in the fabric stout ;
And the perfect pattern was marred for aye
By the one small stitch that was dropped that day.

One small life in God's great plan,
 How futile it seems as the ages roll,
Do what it may, or strive how it can
 To alter the sweep of the infinite whole !
A single stitch in an endless web,
A·drop in the ocean's flow and ebb !
But the pattern is rent where the stitch is lost,
Or marred where the tangled threads have crossed ;
And each life that fails of its true intent
Mars the perfect plan that its Master meant.

REPLY.

"WHAT, then, is Love?" she said.
    Love is a music, blent in curious key
    Of jarring discords and of harmony ;
'T is a delicious draught which, as you sip,
Turns sometimes into poison on your lip.
It is a sunny sky infolding storm,
The fire to ruin or the fire to warm ;
A garland of fresh roses fair to sight,
Which then becomes a chain and fetters tight.
It is a half-heard secret told to two,
A life-long puzzle or a guiding clew,
The joy of joys, the deepest pain of pain ; —
All these Love has been and will be again.

  "How may I know?" she said.
Thou mayest *not* know, for Love has conned the art
To blind the reason and befool the heart.
So subtle is he, not himself may guess

Whether he shall be more or shall be less;
Wrapped in a veil of many colored mists,
He flits disguisèd wheresoe'er he lists,
And for the moment is the thing he seems,
The child of vagrant hope and fairy dreams;
Sails like a rainbow bubble on the wind,
Now high, now low, before us or behind;
And only when our fingers grasp the prize,
Changes his form and swiftly vanishes.

 " Then best not love," she said.
Dear child, there is no better and no best;
Love comes not, bides not at thy slight behest.
As well might thy frail fingers seek to stay
The march of waves in yonder land-locked bay,
As stem the surging tide which ebbs and fills
Mid human energies and human wills.
The moon leads on the strong, resisting sea;
And so the moon of love shall beckon thee,
And at her bidding thou wilt leap and rise,
And follow o'er strange seas, 'neath unknown skies,
Unquestioning; to dash, or soon or late,
On sand or cruel crag, as is thy fate.

"Then woe is me !" she said.
Weep not ; there is a harder, sadder thing, —
Never to know this sweetest suffering !
Never to see the sun, though suns may slay,
Or share the richer feast as others may.
Sooner the sealed and closely guarded wine
Shall seek again its purple clustered vine,
Sooner the attar be again the rose,
Than Love unlearn the secret that it knows !
Abide thy fate, whether for good or ill ;
Fearlessly wait, and be thou certain still,
Whether as foe disguised or friendly guest
He comes, Love's coming is of all things best.

TALITHA CUMI.

UR little one was sick, and the sickness pressed
her sore.
We sat beside her bed, and we felt her hands
and head,
And in our hearts we prayed this one prayer o'er and
o'er:
" Come to us, Christ the Lord; utter thine old-time
word,
'Talitha cumi !' "

And as the night wore on, and the fever flamed more
high,
And a new look burned and grew in the eyes of tender
blue,
Still louder in our hearts uprose the voiceless cry,
" O Lord of love and might, say once again to-night,
'Talitha cumi !' "

And then, and then — he came; we saw him not, but
    felt.
  And he bent above the child, and she ceased to moan,
    and smiled;
And although we heard no sound, as around the bed we
    knelt,
  Our souls were made aware of a mandate in the air,
        " Talitha cumi ! "

And as at dawn's fair summons faded the morning star,
  Holding the Lord's hand close, the child we loved
    arose,
And with him took her way to a country far away;
  And we would not call her dead, for it was his voice
    that said,
        " Talitha cumi ! "

THE BETTER WAY.

WHO serves his country best?
Not he who, for a brief and stormy space,
Leads forth her armies to the fierce affray.
Short is the time of turmoil and unrest,
Long years of peace succeed it and replace :
There is a better way.

Who serves his country best?
Not he who guides her senates in debate,
And makes the laws which are her prop and stay ;
Not he who wears the poet's purple vest,
And sings her songs of love and grief and fate :
There is a better way.

He serves his country best,
Who joins the tide that lifts her nobly on ;
For speech has myriad tongues for every day,
And song but one ; and law within the breast
Is stronger than the graven law on stone :
There is a better way.

He serves his country best
Who lives pure life, and doeth righteous deed,
And walks straight paths, however others stray,
And leaves his sons as uttermost bequest
A stainless record which all men may read :
    This is the better way.

No drop but serves the slowly lifting tide,
No dew but has an errand to some flower,
No smallest star but sheds some helpful ray,
And man by man, each giving to all the rest,
Makes the firm bulwark of the country's power :
    There is no better way.

FOREVER.

THEY sat together in the sun,
  And Youth and Hope stood hovering near;
Like dropping bell-notes one by one
Chimed the glad moments soft and clear;
And still amid their happy speech
The lovers whispered each to each,
      " Forever ! "

Youth spread his wings of rainbow light,
  " Farewell ! " he whispered as he went;
They heeded not nor mourned his flight,
  Wrapped in their measureless content;
And still they smiled, and still was heard
The confidently uttered word,
      " Forever ! "

Hope stayed, her steadfast smile was sweet, —
  Until the even-time she stayed;

Then with reluctant, noiseless feet
   She stole into the solemn shade.
A graver shape moved gently by,
   And bent, and murmured warningly,
      " Forever ! "

And then — where sat the two, sat one !
   No voice spoke back, no glance replied.
Behind her, where she rested lone,
   Hovered the spectre, solemn-eyed ;
She met his look without a thrill,
   And, smiling faintly, whispered still,
      " Forever ! "

Oh, sweet, sweet Youth ! Oh, fading Hope !
   Oh, eyes by tearful mists made blind !
Oh, hands which vainly reach and grope
   For a familiar touch and kind !
Time pauseth for no lover's kiss ;
   Love for its solace has but this, —
      " Forever ! "

MIRACLE.

H ! not in strange portentous way
    Christ's miracles were wrought of old,
The common thing, the common clay,
·He touched and tinctured, and straightway
    It grew to glory manifold.

The barley loaves were daily bread,
    Kneaded and mixed with usual skill;
No care was given, no spell was said,
But when the Lord had blessed, they fed
    The multitude upon the hill.

The hemp was sown 'neath common sun,
    Watered by common dews and rain,
Of which the fishers' nets were spun;
Nothing was prophesied or done
    To mark it from the other grain.

Coarse, brawny hands let down the net
   When the Lord spake and ordered so ;
They hauled the meshes, heavy-wet,
Just as in other days, and set
   Their backs to labor, bending low ;

But quivering, leaping from the lake
   The marvellous, shining burdens rise
Until the laden meshes break,
And, all amazèd, no man spake,
   But gazed with wonder in his eyes.

So still, dear Lord, in every place
   Thou standest by the toiling folk
With love and pity in thy face,
And givest of thy help and grace
   To those who meekly bear the yoke.

Not by strange sudden change and spell,
   Baffling and darkening Nature's face ;
Thou takest the things we know so well
And buildest on them thy miracle, —
   The heavenly on the commonplace.

The lives which seem so poor, so low,
   The hearts which are so cramped and dull,
The baffled hopes, the impulse slow,
Thou takest, touchest all, and lo !
   They blossom to the beautiful.

We need not wait for thunder-peal
   Resounding from a mount of fire,
While round our daily paths we feel
Thy sweet love and thy power to heal,
   Working in us thy full desire.

CHARLOTTE BRONTË.

ORCHID, chance-sown among the moorland
    heather,
    Scarce seen or tasted by the infrequent bee,
Set mid rough mountain growths, lashed by wild
    weather,
    With none to foster thee.

We watch thee fronting all the blasts of heaven,
    Thy slender rootlets grappled fast to rock,
Enduring from thy morning to thy even
    The buffet and the shock.

Never thy sun vouchsafed a cloudless shining,
    Never the wind was tempered to thy pain;
No cloud turned out for thee its silver lining,
    No rainbow followed rain.

Nourished mid hardness, learning patience slowly
    As hearts must do which know no other food,
Duty and Memory, companions holy,
    Shared thy bleak solitude.

Cold touch of Memory, strong chill hand of Duty,
  These held thee fast and ruled thee to the end,
Until, with smile mysterious in its beauty,
  Came Death, rewarding friend.

Earth gave thee scanty cheer, but earth is ended,
  Finished the years of thwarted sacrifice.
We see thee walking forward, well attended,
  Led into Paradise !

Heaven is twice Heaven to one who, hungry-hearted,
  Goes thither knowing no satisfaction here ;
And when we thank the Lord for those departed
  In this sure faith and fear,

We think of thee, lonely no more forever,
  And tasting, while the eternal years unroll,
That joy of Heaven, which like a flowing river
  Satisfies every soul.

END AND MEANS.

E spend our strength in labor day by day,
  We find new strength replacing old alway ;
  And still we cheat ourselves, and still we say :

" No man would work except to win some prize ;
We work to turn our hopes to certainties, —
For gold, or gear, or favor in men's eyes."

And all the while the goal toward which we strain —
Up hill and down, in sunshine and in rain,
Heedless of toil, if so we may attain —

Is but a lure, a heavenly-set decoy
To exercised endeavor, full employ
Of every power, which is man's highest joy.

And work becomes the end, reward the means,
To woo us from our idleness and dreams ;
And each is truly what the other seems.

So, Lord, with such poor service as we do,
Thy full salvation is our prize in view,
For which we long, and which we press unto.

Like a great star on which we fix our eyes,
It dazzles from the high, blue distances,
And seems to beckon and to say, " Arise ! "

And we arise and follow the hard way,
Winning a little nearer day by day,
Our hearts going faster than our footsteps may ;

And never guess the secret sweet device
Which lures us on and upward to the skies,
And makes each toil its own reward and prize.

To give our little selves to thee, to blend
Our weakness with thy strength, O Lord our Friend,
This is life's truest privilege and end.

COMFORTED.

THE last sweet flowers are dying,
　　The last green leaves are red ;
　The wild geese southward flying,
　By law mysterious led,
　Scream noisily o'erhead ;
The honey-bees have hived them,
The butterflies have shrived them ;
　All hushed the song and twitter
And flutter of glad wing ; —
　How could we bear the autumn
If t' were not for the spring?

To see the summer banished,
　Nor dare to bid her stay ;
To mourn o'er beauty vanished
　And joyance driven away ;
　To mark the shortening day ;
To note the sad winds plaining,

The storm cloud and the raining;
  To see the frost lance stabbing
Each faint and wounded thing; —
  Oh, we should hate the autumn
Excepting for the spring!

To know that life is failing
  And pulses beating slow;
To catch the unavailing
  Sad monotones of woe
  All the earth over go;
To know that snows must cover
The grave of friend and lover,
  To hide them from the eyes and hands
That still caress and cling; —
  The heart would break in autumn
If there were not a spring!

For every sleep a waking,
  For every shade a sun,
A balm for each heart breaking,
  A rest for labor done,
  A life by death begun;

And so in wintry weather,
With smile and sigh together,
  We look beyond the present pain,
The daily loss and sting,
  And welcome in the autumn
For the sure hope of spring.

WORDS.

A LITTLE, tender word,
  Wrapped in a little rhyme,
Sent out upon the passing air,
As seeds are scattered everywhere
  In the sweet summer-time.

A little, idle word,
  Breathed in an idle hour;
Between two laughs that word was said,
Forgotten as soon as uttered,
  And yet the word had power.

Away they sped, the words :
  One, like a wingèd seed,
Lit on a soul which gave it room,
And straight began to bud and bloom
  In lovely word and deed.

The other careless word,
  Borne on an evil air,

Found a rich soil, and ripened fast
Its rank and poisonous growths, and cast
  Fresh seeds to work elsewhere.

The speakers of the words
  Passed by and marked, one day,
The fragrant blossoms dewy wet,
The baneful flowers thickly set
  In clustering array.

And neither knew his word;
  One smiled, and one did sigh.
" How strange and sad," one said, "it is
  People should do such things as this !
  I 'm glad it was not I."

And, " What a wondrous word
  To reach so far, so high ! "
The other said, " What joy 't would be
 To send out words so helpfully !
  I wish that it were I."

INFLUENCE.

OUCHED in the rocky lap of hills,
　　The lake's blue waters gleam,
And thence in linked and measured rills
　Down to the valley stream,
To rise again, led higher and higher,
And slake the city's hot desire.

High as the lake's bright ripples shine,
　　So high the water goes,
But not a drop that air-drawn line
　　Passes or overflows;
Though man may strive and man may woo,
The stream to its own law is true.

Vainly the lonely tarn its cup
　　Holds to the feeding skies;
Unless the source be lifted up,
　　The streamlet cannot rise:
By law inexorably blent,
Each is the other's measurement.

Ah, lonely tarn ! ah, striving rill !
So yearn these souls of ours,
And beat with sad and urgent will
Against the unheeding powers.
In vain is longing, vain is force ;
No stream goes higher than its source.

AN EASTER SONG.

SONG of sunshine through the rain,
 Of spring across the snow,
A balm to heal the hurts of pain,
 A peace surpassing woe.
Lift up your heads, ye sorrowing ones,
 And be ye glad of heart,
For Calvary and Easter Day,
Earth's saddest day and gladdest day,
 Were just one day apart!

With shudder of despair and loss
 The world's deep heart was wrung,
As lifted high upon his cross
 The Lord of Glory hung,
When rocks were rent, and ghostly forms
 Stole forth in street and mart;
But Calvary and Easter Day,
Earth's blackest day and whitest day,
 Were just one day apart!

No hint or whisper stirred the air
　To tell what joy should be ;
The sad disciples, grieving there,
　'Nor help nor hope could see.
Yet all the while the glad, near sun
　Made ready its swift dart,
And Calvary and Easter Day,
The darkest day and brightest day,
　Were just one day apart !

Oh, when the strife of tongues is loud,
　And the heart of hope beats low,
When the prophets prophesy of ill,
　And the mourners come and go,
In this sure thought let us abide,
　And keep and stay our heart, —
That Calvary and Easter Day,
Earth's heaviest day and happiest day,
　Were but one day apart !

SO LONG AGO.

THEY stood upon the vessel's deck
    To catch our farewell look and beck.
    Two girlish figures, fair and frail,
Hovering against a great white sail
Like spirit shapes in dazzling air, —
I seem to see them standing there,
Always together, always so, —
'T was long ago, oh, long ago!

The east was bright with yellow noon,
The flying vessel vanished soon.
Flashes of jubilant white spray
Beckoned and pointed her the way.
A lessening speck she outward sped;
Sadly we turned, but still we said,
"They will come back again, we know," —
'T was long ago, so long ago!

Those faces sweet, those happy eyes,
Looked nevermore on Western skies;
Where the hot sunbeams weave their net
O'er cedar-crowned, sad Olivet,
They who had shared their lives shared death,
Tasting at once the first strange breath
Of those quick airs for souls that flow
So long ago, so long ago!

In vain we picture to our eyes
The convent gray, the still, blue skies,
The mountain with its bordering wood; —
Still do they stand as then they stood,
Hovering like spirits fair and frail
Against the dazzle of the sail;
The red lips part, the faces glow,
As long ago, so long ago!

A BIRTHDAY.

WHAT shall I do to keep your day,
    My darling, dead for many a year?
    I could not, if I would, forget
   It is your day; and yet, and yet —
It is so hard to find a way
    To keep it, now you are not here.

I cannot add the lightest thing
    To the full sum of happiness
    Which now is yours; nor dare I try
    To frame a wish for you, since I
Am blind to know, as weak to bring,
    All impotent to aid or bless.

And yet it is your day, and so,
    Unlike all other days, one bead
    Of gold in the long rosary
    Of dull beads little worth to me.
And I must keep it bright, and show
    That what is yours is dear indeed.

How shall I keep it here alone? —
 With prayers in which your name is set;
 With smiles, not tears; and sun, not rain;
 With memories sweeter far than pain,
With tender backward glances thrown,
 And far on-lookings, clearer yet.

The gift I would have given to you,
 And which you cannot need or take,
 Shall still be given; and it shall be
 A secret between you and me, —
A sweet thought, every birthday new,
 That it is given for your sake.

And so your day, yours safely still,
 Shall come and go with ebbing time, —
 The day of all the year most sweet, —
 Until the years so slow, so fleet,
Shall bring me, as in time they will,
 To where all days are yours and mine.

DERELICT.

BANDONED wrecks they plunge and drift,
   The sport of sea and wind,
The tempest drives, the billows lift,
The aimless sails they flap and shift
   With impulse vague and blind,
As tossing on from wave to wave
They seek — and shun — the yawning grave.

The decks once trodden by busy feet
   Man nevermore shall tread;
The cargoes brave of wine or wheat,
Now soaked with salt and drenched with sleet,
   And mixed and scatterèd,
No merchant shall appraise or buy
Or store in vat or granary.

The wet ropes pull the creaking sails,
   As though by hands drawn tight.
Echoes the hold with ghostly wails,
While daylight wanes, and twilight pales,
   And drops the heavy night,

And vast and silent fish swim by,
And scan the wreck with cruel eye.

Ha! lights ahead!   A ship is near!
    The dumb wreck makes no sign;
No lantern shows, returns no cheer,
But straight and full, without a veer,
    Sped by the urging brine
She goes — a crash! her errand done,
The deadly, lonely thing drives on.

Oh, hopeless lives, distorted, crushed,
    Which, like the lonely wreck,
Lashed by the waves and tempest-tossed,
With rudder gone and cargo lost,
    Torn ribs and leaking deck,
Plunge on through sunshine and eclipse,
A menace to the happier ships.

All oceans know them, and all lands.
    Speechless they drift us by;
To questioning voices, friendly hands,
Warnings or counsels or commands,
    Still making no reply.
God send them help if help may be,
Or sink them harmless in his sea.

H. H.

HAT was she most like? Was she like the wind,
Fresh always, and untired; intent to find
New fields to penetrate, new heights to gain;
Scattering all mists with sudden, radiant wing;
Stirring the languid pulses; quickening
The apathetic mood, the weary brain?

Or was she like the sun, whose gift of cheer
Endureth for all seasons of the year,
Alike in winter's cold or summer's heat?
Or like the sea, which brings its gifts from far,
And still, wherever want and straitness are,
Lays down a sudden largess at their feet?

Or was she like a wood, where light and shade,
And sound and silence, mingle unafraid;
Where mosses cluster, and, in coverts dark,

Shy blossoms court the brief and wandering air,
Mysteriously sweet; and here and there
  A firefly flashes like a sudden spark?

Or like a wilful brook, which laughs and leaps
All unexpectedly, and never keeps
  The course predicted, as it seaward flows?
Or like a stream-fed river, brimming high?
Or like a fruit, where those who love descry
  A pungent charm no other flavor knows?

I cannot find her type.   In her were blent
Each varied and each fortunate element
  Which souls combine, with something all her own.
Sadness and mirthfulness, a chorded strain,
The tender heart, the keen and searching brain,
  The social zest, the power to live alone.

Comrade of comrades, giving man the slip
To seek in Nature truest comradeship;
  Tenacity and impulse ruled her fate,
This grasping firmly what that flashed to feel, —
The velvet scabbard and the sword of steel,
  The gift to strongly love, to frankly hate!

Patience as strong as was her hopefulness ;
A joy in living which grew never less
   As years went on and age drew gravely nigh ;
Vision which pierced the veiling mists of pain,
And saw beyond the mortal shadows plain
   The eternal day-dawn broadening in the sky.

The love of Doing, and the scorn of Done ;
The playful fancy, which, like glinting sun,
   No chill could daunt, no loneliness could smother.
Upon her ardent pulse Death's chillness lies ;
Closed the brave lips, the merry, questioning eyes.
   She was herself ! — there is not such another.

FREEDOM.

WOULD be free ! For freedom is all fair,
  And her strong smile is like the smile of God.
  Her voice rings out like trumpet on the air,
  And men rise up and follow ; though the road
Be all unknown and hard to understand,
They tread it gladly, holding Freedom's hand.

I would be free ! The little spark of Heaven
  Let in my soul when life was breathed in me
Is like a flame, this way and that way driven
  By ever wavering winds, which ceaselessly
Kindle and blow till all my soul is hot,
And would consume if liberty were not.

I would be free ! But what is freedom, then?
  For widely various are the shapes she wears
In different ages and to different men ;
  And many titles, many forms she bears, —
Riot and revolution, sword and flame,
All called in turn by Freedom's honored name.

I would be free ! Not free to burn and spoil,
  To trample down the weak and smite the strong,
To seize the larger share of wine and oil,
  And rob the sun my daylight to prolong,
And rob the night of sleep while others wake, —
Feast on their famine, basely free to take.

I would be free ! Free in a dearer way,
  Free to become all that I may or can ;
To be my best and utmost self each day,
  Not held or bound by any chain of man,
By dull convention, or by foolish sneer,
Or love's mistaken clasp of feeble fear.

Free to be kind and true and faithful ; free
  To do the happy thing that makes life good,
To grow as grows the goodly forest-tree ;
  By none gainsaid, by none misunderstood,
To taste life's freshness with a child's delight,
And find new joy in every day and night.

I would be free ! Ah ! so may all be free.
  Then shall the world grow sweet at core and sound,
And, moved in blest and ordered circuit, see
  The bright millennial sun rise fair and round,
Heaven's day begin, and Christ, whose service is
Freedom all n

THE VISION AND THE SUMMONS.

THE trance of golden afternoon
   Lay on the Judæan skies ;
The trance of vision, like a swoon,
   Sealed the Apostle's eyes.
Upon the roof he sat and saw
Angelic hands let down and draw
Again the mighty vessel full
Of beasts and birds innumerable.

Three times the heavenly vision fell,
   Three times the Lord's voice spoke ;
When Peter, loath to break the spell,
   Roused from his trance, and woke,
To hear a common sound and rude,
Which jarred and shook his solitude, —
A knocking at the doorway near,
Where stood the two from Cæsarea.

And should he heed, or should he stay?
   Scarce had the vision fled, —
Perchance it might return that day,
   Perchance more words be said
By the Lord's voice? — he rises slow;
Again the knocking; he must go;
Nor guessed, while going down the stair,
That 't was the Lord who called him there.

Had he sat still upon the roof,
   Wooing the vision long,
The Gentile world had missed the truth,
   And Heaven one " sweet new song."
Souls might have perished in blind pain,
And the Lord Christ have died in vain
For them.   He knew not what it meant,
But Peter rose and Peter went.

Oh, souls which sit in upper air,
   Longing for heavenly sight,
Glimpses of truth all fleeting-fair,
   Set in unearthly light, —
Is there no knocking heard below,
For which you should arise and go,

Leaving the vision, and again
Bearing its message unto men?

Sordid the world were vision not,
　But fruitless were your stay;
So, having seen the sight, and got
　The message, haste away.
Though pure and bright thy higher air,
And hot the street and dull the stair,
Still get thee down, for who shall know
But 't is the Lord who knocks below?

FORECAST.

LWAYS when the roses bloom most brightly,
   Some sad heart is sure to presage blight ;
   Always when the breeze is kindliest blowing
   There are eyes that look out for a gale ;
Always when the bosom's lord sits lightly
   Comes some croaking proverb to affright,
And in sweetest music grieving blindly
   Sits the shadow of a sorrow pale.

Though to-day says not a word to sadden,
   Still to-morrow's menace fills my ear.
Less intent on this than that I hie me,
   Fearful, eager, all the worst to know,
Missing that which might the moment gladden,
   For the prescience of a far-off fear,
Which again and yet again flits by me,
   Clouding all the sunshine as I go.

There is manna for the day's supplying,
　There are daily dews and daily balms,
Yet I shrink and shudder to remember
　All the desert drought I yet may see.
Past the green oasis fare I, sighing,
　Caring not to rest beneath the palms.
All my May is darkened by December,
　All my laughter by the tears to be.

Must my life go on thus to its closing?
　Lord, hold fast this restless heart of mine;
Put thy arm about me when I shiver,
　Make me feel thy presence all the way.
Hope and fear, and travail and reposing,
　All by thee are cared for, all are thine,
Quick to help, sufficient to deliver,
　Near in sun and shade, in night and day.

EARLY TAKEN.

HE seemed so young, so young to die !
Life, like a dawning, rosy day,
Stretched from her fair young feet away,
And beams from the just-risen sun
Beckoned and wooed and urged her on.
She met the light with happy eyes,
Fresh with the dews of Paradise,
And held her sweet hands out to grasp
The joys that crowded to her clasp,
Each a surprise, and all so dear :
How could we guess that night was near?

She seemed so young, so young to die !
When the old go, we sadly say,
'T is Nature's own appointed way ;
The ripe grain gathered in must be,
The ripe fruit from the laden tree,
The sear leaf quit the bare, brown bough ;
Summer is done, 't is autumn now,

God's harvest-time ; the sheaves among,
His angels raise the reaping-song,
And though we grieve, we would not stay
The shining sickles on their way.

She seemed so young, so young to die !
We question wearily and vain
What never answer shall make plain :
" Can it be this the good Lord meant
Which frustrates his benign intent?
Why was she planted like a flower
In mortal sun and mortal shower,
And left to grow, and taught to bloom,
To gather beauty and perfume ;
Why were we set to train and tend
If only for this bootless end?"

She seemed so young, so young to die !
But age and youth, — what do they mean
Measured by the eternal scheme
Of God, and sifted out and laid
In his unerring scales and weighed?
How may we test their sense or worth, —
These poor glib phrases, born of earth,

False accents of a long exile, —
Or know the angels do not smile,
Holding out truth's immortal gauge,
To hear us prate of youth and age?

  She seemed so young, so young to die !
So needed here by every one,
Nor there ; for heaven has need of none.
And yet, how can we tell or say?
Heaven is so far, so far away !
How do we know its blissful store
Is full and needeth nothing more?
It may be that some tiny space
Lacked just that little angel face,
Or the full sunshine missed one ray
Until our darling found the way.

SOME LOVER'S DEAR THOUGHT.

OUGHT to be kinder always,
　　For the light of his kindly eyes ;
I ought to be wiser always,
　Because he is so just and wise ;
And gentler in all my bearing,
And braver in all my daring,
　For the patience that in him lies.

I must be as true as the Heaven
　While he is as true as the day,
Nor balance the gift with the given,
　For he giveth to me alway.
And I must be firm and steady ;
For my Love, he is that already,
　And I follow him as I may.

O dear little golden fetter,
　You bind me to difficult things ;

But my soul while it strives grows better,
    And I feel the stirring of wings
As I stumble, doubting and dreading,
Up the path of his stronger treading,
    Intent on his beckonings.

ASHES.

SAW the gardener bring and strew
 Gray ashes where blush roses grew.
The fair, still roses bent them low,
 Their pink cheeks dimpled all with dew,
And seemed to view with pitying air
The dim gray atoms lying there.
 Ah, bonny rose, all fragrances,
 And life and hope and quick desires,
 What can you need or gain from these
Poor ghosts of long-forgotten fires?
 The rose-tree leans, the rose-tree sighs,
 And wafts this answer subtly wise :
" All death, all life are mixed and blent,
Out of dead lives fresh life is sent,
 Sorrow to these is growth for me,
 And who shall question God's decree?"

Ah, dreary life, whose gladsome spark
   No longer leaps in song and fire,
But lies in ashes gray and stark,
   Defeated hopes and dead desire,
Useless and dull and all bereft, —
Take courage, this one thing is left :
   Some happier life may use thee so,
Some flower bloom fairer on its tree,
   Some sweet or tender thing may grow
To stronger life because of thee ;
   Content to play a humble part,
   Give of the ashes of thy heart,
And haply God, whose dear decrees
Taketh from those to give to these,
   Who draws the snow-drop from the snows
   May from those ashes feed a rose.

ONE LESSER JOY.

HAT is the dearest happiness of heaven?
　　　Ah, who shall say !
　So many wonders, and so wondrous fair,
　Await the soul who, just arrivèd there
In trance of safety, sheltered and forgiven,
　Opens glad eyes to front the eternal day :

Relief from earth's corroding discontent,
　　　Relief from pain,
　The satisfaction of perplexing fears,
　Full compensation for the long, hard years,
Full understanding of the Lord's intent,
　The things that were so puzzling made quite plain ;

And all astonished joy as, to the spot,
　　　From further skies,
　Crowd our belovèd with white wingèd feet,
　And voices than the chiming harps more sweet,

Faces whose fairness we had half forgot,
  And outstretched hands, and welcome in their eyes ; —

Heart cannot image forth the endless store
          We may but guess ;
  But this one lesser joy I hold my own :
  All shall be known in heaven ; at last be known
The best and worst of me ; the less, the more,
  My own shall know — and shall not love me less.

Oh, haunting shadowy dread which underlies
          All loving here !
  We inly shiver as we whisper low,
" Oh, if they knew — if they could only know,
Could see our naked souls without disguise —
  How they would shrink from us and pale with fear ! "

The bitter thoughts we hold in leash within
          But do not kill ;
  The petty anger and the mean desire,
  The jealousy which burns, — a smouldering fire, —
The slimy trail of half-unnoted sin,
  The sordid wish which daunts the nobler will.

We fight each day with foes we dare not name.
　　　　We fight, we fail !
　　Noiseless the conflict and unseen of men ;
　　We rise, are beaten down, and rise again,
And all the time we smile, we move, the same,
　　And even to dearest eyes draw close the veil.

But in the blessed heaven these wars are past ;
　　　　Disguise is o'er !
　　With new anointed vision, face to face,
　　We shall see all, and clasped in close embrace
Shall watch the haunting shadow flee at last,
　　And know as we are known, and fear no more.

CLOSE AT HAND.

"DID you not know Me, my child?" the lips and eyes that were all love seemed to say to her. "You have thought the thoughts that I inspired, you have spoken my words, you set forth to fight on my side in the battle against evil; and yet you forget me, and have often gone near to deny me, while I was standing by your side and giving you the strength to speak and think. Look at me now, and see if I am not better than the images that have hid me from you." — *A Doubting Heart.*

THE day is long, and the day is hard;
　　We are tired of the march and of keeping guard,
　　Tired of the sense of a fight to be won,
Of days to live through and of work to be done,
Tired of ourselves and of being alone.

And all the while, did we only see,
We walk in the Lord's own company;
We fight, but 'tis he who nerves our arm,
He turns the arrows which else might harm,
And out of the storm he brings a calm.

The work which we count so hard to do,
He makes it easy, for he works too ;
The days that are long to live are his,
A bit of his bright eternities,
And close to our need his helping is.

O eyes that were holden and blinded quite,
And caught no glimpse of the guiding light !
O deaf, deaf ears which did not hear
The heavenly garment trailing near !
O faithless heart, which dared to fear !

ONLY A DREAM.

DREAMED we sat within a shaded place,
　　Where mournful waters fell, and no sun shone ;
And suddenly, a smile upon his face,
　There came to us a winged, mysterious one,
And said, with pitying eyes : " O mourning souls, arise !

" Take up your travelling staves, your sandals lace,
　And journey to the Northland and the snow,
Where wild and leaping Borealis trace
　Fantastic, glistening dances to and fro ;
Where suns at midnight beam, to fright the sleeper's
　　　dream.

" There, in the icy, solitary waste,
　God's goodness grants this boon,— that thou shalt see,
And hold communion for a little space·
　With that dear child so lately gone from thee.
Arise, and haste away ; God may not let her stay."

So we arose, and quickly we went forth ;
   How could we slight such all undreamed-of boon ?
And when we reached the ultimate far North —
   All in a hush of frozen afternoon,
Lit by a dim sun-ray, liker to night than day —

There, o'er the white bare feld we saw her come,
   Our little maid, in the dear guise we knew,
With the same look she used to wear at home,
   The same sweet eyes of deepest, dark-fringed blue ;
Her steps they made no sound upon the icy ground.

She kissed us gently, and she stood and smiled,
   While close we clasped and questioned her, and strove
To win some hint or answer from the child
   That should appease the hunger of our love,
Something to soothe the pain when she must go again.

And was she happy, happier than of old ?
   Did heaven fulfil its promises of bliss ?
And had she seen our other dead, and told
   The story of that loving faithfulness
Which held them dearly yet and never would forget ?

To all these questions she made no replies :
   She only smiled a softly wistful smile,

And looked with gentle eyes into our eyes,
　　And kissed us back ; and in a little while
She said, " Now I must go ; my Lady told me so."

Then jealously we cried : " What is the name
　　Of this thy ' Lady ' ?　Is she good to thee ?
Has she above all other angels claim
　　To thine obedience, dear ; or can it be
The Mother of our Lord ? "　She answered not a word !

But sighed, and laid her finger on her lips,
　　And kissed us all, and straightway from our sight,
As twilight wanes and melts in night's eclipse,
　　She vanished, and we looked to left and right,
And wildly called her name, but, oh ! no answer came.

And with the anguished call the vision broke,
　　The equal sky of summer shone o'erhead ;
The earliest birds were singing as I woke, —
　　All was a dream, except that she was dead,
And that familiar pain I tasted once again.

Thank God, it was a dream !　How could we bear
　　To see her stand with wistful eyes down bent,
In the old likeness that she used to wear,
　　And know her sad and only half-content,
And shy and puzzled even, as if not used to heaven ?

Better, far better, not to know or see !
   O Lord, whose faithfulness all ages prove,
We trust the darling of our hearts to thee,
   Asking no explanations of thy love ;
Keep thou her safe alway, and give her back some day.

AT THE ALTAR.

 KNEEL before thine altar, Lord, and fain a gift
would bring,
But all I have is worthless and unfit for offering;
A foolish heart, a foolish dream, a foolish, fruitless pain, —
Such are my all; O Love of Love, do not the gift disdain !

And even as earthly monarchs do, who take the tribute
given,
And quick restore, by royal grace increased to seven times
seven,
So take, O Lord, my offering, and vouchsafe me presently,
For emptiness thy fulness, for my hunger thy supply.

I lay my heart down at thy feet, that tired heart and old,
Whose youthful throb has grown so faint, whose youthful
fire so cold ;
Heart of the world's heart, Lord of joy, and mighty Lord
of pain,
Take thou the gift, and quicken it, and give it back again.

My foolish dream, so dear, so prized, baptized in many
 tears,
Loved even as sickly children are, the more for doubts and
 fears,
O Lord, whose word is faithfulness eternal to endure,
Take it ; and give me, in its stead, the Hope that standeth
 sure.

The pain, that half was baffled will, which could not bear
 to die,
And, stilled by day, would stir by night and wake me with
 its cry,
That pain so close, so intimate, that Death could scarce
 destroy,
I leave it, Lord, before thy feet ; give me instead thy joy.

All empty-handed came I in, full-handed forth I go ;
Go thou beside me, Lord of Grace, and keep me ever so.
Thanks are poor things for such wide good, but all my life
 is thine, —
Thou who hast turned my stones to bread, my water into
 wine.

ETERNITY.

LITTLE waves, which kiss the sands
  With cool, caressing lips of foam,
  And murmurs soft, and outstretched hands,
Like glad, tired children nearing home,
O little waves, so soft, so small,
How are you linked, if linked at all,
To those mid-ocean billows strong,
By fierce winds scourged and driven along,
Tossed up to heaven, and then again
Sucked in black gulfs of whelming main ;
Never at rest and never spent?
Urged by a speeding discontent,
A seething strife which knows not ease,
Are you akin to such as these?
The little waves they flash and rise,
  And lisp this answer wonderingly,
With laughter in their glancing eyes :
  "They are the sea — we are the sea."

O small, spent waves of surging time,
　　Which break and fall upon life's shore
With soft and intermittent chime,
　　A moment seen, then seen no more,
How are you linked, if linked you be,
To that great dark eternity
Which stretches far beyond our gaze,
And rounds our nights and rounds our days?
We see its darkling billows flow,
But dare not follow where they go,
Nor guess what distance dim and vast
They span to find a shore at last.
O little waves, what share have ye
In this great dim eternity?
The fleet waves answer as they run :
　　" Or near, or far, one name have we,
Time and eternity are one ;
　　It is the sea — we are the sea."

RÉSTFULNESS.

ONG time my restless wishes fought and strove,
    Long time I bent me to the heavy task
Of winning such full recompense of love
    As dream could paint, importunate fancy ask.

Morning and night a hunger filled my soul;
    Ever my eager hands went out to sue;
And still I sped toward a shifting goal,
    And still the horizon widened as I flew.

There was no joy in love, but jealous wrath;
    I walked athirst all day, and did not heed
The wayside brooks which followed by my path
    And held their cooling threadlets to my need.

But now, these warring fancies left behind,
    I sit in clear air with the sun o'erhead,
And take my share, repining not, and find
    Perpetual feast in just such daily bread:

Asking no more than what unasked is sent ;
  Freedom is dearer still than love may be ;
And I, my dearest, am at last content,
  Content to love thee and to leave thee free.

Love me then not, for pity nor for prayer,
  But as the sunshine loveth and the rain,
Which speed them gladly through the upper air
  Because the gracious pathway is made plain.

And as we watch the slant lines, gold and dun,
  Bridge heaven's distance all intent to bless,
And cavil not if we or other one
  Shall have the larger portion or the less,

So with unvexèd eye I mark and see
  Where blessed and blessing your sweet days are spent ;
And though another win more love from thee,
  Having my share I am therewith content.

IN AND ON.

On earth as *in* heaven. — *The Lord's Prayer.*

N earth we take but feeble hold ;
    Joy is not confident or bold ;
    We dare not strike deep roots and stay,
Nor trust to-morrow or to-day.
We scatter grain beneath frail skies,
And note its shoot and watch its rise,
And do not know or guess a whit
What other hands shall garner it.
We raise our songs, but fast and soon
Our voices unto silence die,
And other voices end the tune
Which, too, shall falter presently.
"Forever" is our idle oath ;
But while the word is on our lip
Night falls, and past and future both
Out of our hold and keeping slip.
We dare not love as angels may,

Lest love should fail us or betray ;
And life goes on and we go hence,
Nor never know continuance.

In heaven is safety and sure peace ;
There is no waning nor decrease.
The endless ages ebb and flow,
The endless harvests riper grow ;
Fast in the rich eternal mould
The heart's deep roots take hold, take hold
With the strong joy of permanence,
Never to be transplanted thence.
Sweet songs are sung to very close,
Sweet closes recommence and blend ;
And still as rose-bud answers rose
The new strains grow, the old strains end.
Forever means forever there ;
New joy past sorrow reconciles,
And hung in clear and golden air
An undeceiving morrow smiles.
While Love the law and Love the sun
Blesses and warms and saves each one ;
And God's dear will, our earthly prayer,
Is made quite plain and perfect there.

A DAY-TIME MOON.

UP in the shining and sun-lighted blue,
　　Where foam-white clouds sail like a fairy fleet,
The pale moon hovers, glimmering wanly
　　　through,
　　Like a sad chord in chorus gay and sweet.

Frailer than cloud she seems, and torn and frayed ;
　　A little wandering fragment, drifting slow,
Of that brave golden summer moon which made
　　Midnight so beautiful awhile ago.

Why comes she back at this untimely hour,
　　When noon is nigh and birds are singing clear,
And the fierce sun, her rival, burns with power ? —
　　What can the poor, the pretty moon want here ?

Does she feel lonely in the peopled sky,
　　The only moon among a starry host ;
They all together in brave company,
　　She wandering solitary as a ghost ?

Or does she grieve that we so soon forget
    The perfect beauty of her tempered ray,
Drowsily praising her sweet beams, but yet
    Keeping our real joyance for the day?

Poor, pallid moon, with a reproachful face
    She eyes the humming world as on it moves,
Yearning through the vast intervening space
    For some one who remembers her and loves.

And like a homesick spirit, sad at heart,
    To heaven's happy ways not wonted yet;
She seems to murmur when she strays apart:
    " I still am faithful ; but you all forget."

A MIDNIGHT SUN.

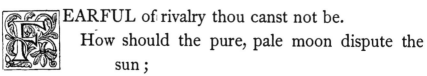EARFUL of rivalry thou canst not be.
    How should the pure, pale moon dispute the
       sun ;
Or the innumerable company
    Of scintillant stars, though banded all as one?

One glance of thy hot anger can dismay
    The boldest planet till he fades and flees,
And hastes to bury his affrighted ray
    In far, uncalculated distances.

Why linger then to rule the midnight sky,
    Baffling celestial rule, and vexing men
Who watched thy sinking but an hour gone by
    Only to see thee turn thy steps again?

The drowsy birds are drooping on the trees,
    The cock's faint crow but dimly prophesies ;
The weary peasant slumbers ill at ease,
    And blinks and winks, half wakes and rubs his eyes.

The east it flushes wanly, as in doubt;
  Foams with unrest the roused and wrathful sea;
The scared moon peeped, then turned her round about,
  And fled across the heavens at sight of thee.

Sovereign of day thou art by law divine,
  None shall thy rulership or sway divide;
The dawning and the rosy morn are thine,
  The busy afternoon and hot noontide.

But dusk of breezy twilight firefly-lit,
  With chirp of drowsy bird and flash of dew,
And children clasping sleep while shunning it,
  And midnight, with its deep, mysterious blue, —

These are the properties and appanage
  Of sovereign Night, thy equal and thy foe;
And when she cometh and flings down her gage
  And claims her kingdom, 't is thy time to go.

And when in turn thou comest she must flee.
  Each has a realm, and each must reign alone;
And not for her remains and not for thee
  To seize and claim an undivided throne.

The sky it loves thee, but it loves the moon ;
   The world it needs thee, but it needs the night.
Blind us not, then, with thine inopportune,
   Bewildering, and unexpected light.

Leave us to sleep, and duly take thy rest.
   Vain is the plea ; the king is on his way,
And, following his tossing golden crest,
   Comes the long train of hours, and it is Day.

HER VOICE.

K. R. J.

WHERE is the voice gone which so many years,
    Each year grown sweeter, rose in glorious song,
  Interpreting to all our hearts and ears
    Ecstasy, passion, pain, the yearning strong
Of baffled love, the patience stronger yet,
The pang of hope, the sweetness of regret?

How should that perish which seemed born of heaven
    And framed to breathe the meaning of the skies?
Can music render back such gift once given;
    Or bear to know some subtlest harmonies
Must evermore go half expressed, perceived,
Forever thwarted and forever grieved?

Heaven did not need her voice; its courts are full
    Of choristers angelic trained for praise.
No note is lacking in the wonderful
    According chorus, which, untired, always

Sings, " Holy, holy, holy ! " round the throne ;
But earth seems dumb to us now it is gone !

God does not grudge us anything of good !
   And I will dare to fancy when she died,
And on the sweet lips which so featly wooed
   Music, the guest, to enter and abide,
Death laid his hand, and with insistence strong
Shut in the secret of their power of song, —

That the dear voice, thus sadly dispossessed
   And reft of home, sped forth upon its road,
And like a lost and lonely child, in quest
   Of shelter, sought another warm abode
In human shape, — some gentle, new-born thing,
Where it might fold its torn and beaten wing.

And if, long years from now, we catch a strain
   Which has the old, familiar, rapturous thrill,
We shall smile, saying, " There it is again !
   It is not dead, it wakes in music still.
Hark ! how the lovely accents soar and float,
A skylark singing from a woman's throat ! "

A FLORENTINE JULIET.

HAT is it, my Renzo?   What is thy desire?
      To hear my story, hear the whole of it?
      And with a shamefaced air and reddened cheek
That " others know it all, and why not thou ? "
Who has been talking to thee of me, then ;
Setting thee on to question and suspect?
Ah, boy, with eyes still full of childish dreams,
And yet with manhood on the firm young lip,
'T is a hard thing to ask me, and a strange !
A woman does not easily lay bare
Her history, which is her very heart,
Even to that piece of her she calls her son !
Son he may be, but still he is a man,
And she, though mother, is a woman still ;
And men and women are made different,
And vainly 'gainst the barrier of sex
They beat and beat, — all their lives long they beat,
And never pass, never quite understand !

Yet must I do this hard thing for thy sake,
Since who shall do it for thee, if not I?
Thy father, who had else more fitly told,
Is at the wars, the weary, wasting wars; —
Long years ago he sailed unto the wars,
And, dead or living, comes not back to us.
Unhappy is the son who, woman-bred,
Knows not the firm feel of a father's hand;
And I, widow or wife, I know not which,
Wofulest widow, still more woful wife!
Must frame my faltering tongue to tell the tale,
And snatch my thoughts back from their present pain
To the old days, the hard and cruel days,
Full of sharp hatred and stern vengeances,
Which yet were beautiful to him and me
Who lived and loved each other and were young;
But unto thee, born in a softer hour,
Come as dim echoes of some warlike peal.

Thou bearest an honorable name, my son,
Two mighty houses meet and blend in thee;
For I, thy mother, of the warlike line
Of Bardi, lords of Florence in past time,
Was daughter, and thy sire Ippolito

Sprang from the Buondelmonti, their sworn foes;
For we were Guelph and they were Ghibelline,
And centuries of wrong, and seas of blood,
And old traditional hatreds sundered us.
Even in my babyhood I heard the name
Of Buondelmonti uttered 'twixt set teeth
And coupled with a curse, and I would pout,
And knit my brows, and clench my tiny fist
And whimper at the very sound of it;
Whereat my father, stout Amérigo,
Would catch me up and toss me overhead,   ·
And swear I was best Bardi of them all;
And if his sons but matched his only maid
They 'd make quick work of the black Ghibellines
And of the Buondelmonti !

     So I grew
To woman's stature, and men called me fair,
And suitors, like a flight of bees, began
To hum and cluster wheresoe'er I moved;
And then there came the day, — that fateful day,
When little Gian, my father's latest born,
Was carried for chrism to the baptistery;
And standing, all unaware, beside the font,

I looked across the dim and crowded church
And saw a face — a dazzling, youthful face !
A face that smote my vision like a star ;
With golden locks, and eyes divinely bright
Like San Michele in the picture there —
Fixed upon mine.

         Had any whispered then
It was Ippolito, our foeman's son,
At whom I gazed, I should have turned away,
My father's daughter sure had turned away.
But nothing warned me, nothing hindered him ;
We looked upon each other, Fate so willed,
And with our eyes our hearts met !

                          " Cursed cur,"
My brother muttered, fingering at his sword,
" I 'll teach you to ogle us when this is done ! "
" Who is it, then ? " I whispered, and he told ;
And with the name I felt my heart like lead
Turn cold and cold and suddenly sink down.

And still that tender, radiant gaze wooed mine,
And still I felt the enchantment burn and burn,
But would not turn my head or look again ;

And all that night I lay and felt those eyes,
And day by day they seemed to follow me,
Like unknown planets of some strange new heaven
Whose depths I dared not question or explore ;
And love and hate so strove for mastery
Within my girl's heart, made their battle-field,
That all my forces failed and life grew faint.

He, for his part, set forth with heart afire
To learn my name, — sad knowledge, easy gained,
Leaving the learner stricken with a chill !
And after that, whenever I might go
To ball or feast, I saw him, only him !
And while the other cavaliers pressed round
To praise my face or dress, or hold my fan,
Or bid me to the dance, he stood aloof
With passionate eyes, but never might draw near.
For still my brother Piero or my sire
Were close behind, with dark set brows intent
To watch him that he did not dare to speak.
Only his eyes met mine, and in my cheeks
I felt the guilty color grow and grow ;
And once, when all were masqued, amid the crowd
A hand touched mine, and oh, I knew 't was his !

At last, with baffling of his heart-sick hope
And long suspense and sorrow, he fell ill ;
And in a moment when life's tide ran low
He told his mother all ; she, loving him well
And loath to see him perish thus forlorn,
Became his ally, spoke him words of cheer,
And with my cousin Contessa, her sworn friend,
She counsel took ; and so, betwixt the two,
It came about that on a day of spring
When almond blossoms whitened the brown boughs
And olives were in bud and all birds sang,
We met, — a meeting cunningly contrived,
In an old villa garden past the walls.
My mother had led me thither, knowing naught,
And I, naught knowing, had wandered for a space
Among the boskage and the fragrant vines,
And, standing by a water-fount of stone
Listening the tinkle and the cool, wet splash
Of the thin drip, and thinking still of him
(For I went thinking of him all the day),
I heard the soft throb of a mandolin,
And next a voice, divinely sweet it seemed,
A voice unheard till then, and yet I knew
The voice for his ; and this the song it sang : —

" Ah, thorns so sharp, so strong !
　Ah, path so hard, so long !
　What do I care?　Thither I fare !
　　My Rose is there !

" Ah, life so dear, so brief !
　Ah, death, the end of grief !
　All I can bear, all will I dare !
　　My Rose is there ! "

The music ceased, the while spell-bound I stayed ;
Then came a rustle, — he was at my feet !

Few moments might we stay, and few words speak ;
But love is swift of tongue ! all was arranged, —
The plan of our escape, the hour, the place,
And that Ippolito, next night but two,
With a rope-ladder hidden 'neath his cloak,
Should stand beneath my window.　Once on ground
A priest should wait to bind us quickly one.
Then a mad gallop, ere the dawn of day,
Would set us safely forth beyond the rule
Of the Black Lily.　Next, as hand in hand
We stood, our lips met in a first long kiss,
And then we parted.

With his vanishing
The thing grew like a dream, and as in dream
I seemed to walk the next day and the next;
For all my thoughts were of that coming night,
And all my fear was lest it should not come.
And all the old-time animosities,
And all the hates bred in me from a child,
And feudal faiths and loyalties were dead, —
I was no more a Bardi; Love ruled all.

It came, the night, and on the stroke of twelve
I stood at casement, wrapped in veil, with mask
And muffling cloak laid ready close beside;
And there I stood and watched, and heard the bells
Strike one, two, three, and saw the rose of dawn
Deepen to day, and still my love came not.

Then, fearing to be spied, I crept to bed;
And lying in a weary trance, half sleep,
Heard shouts and cries and noise of joyful stir
Run through the palace, and quick echoing feet,
And little Cosmo thundering at my door.
" Wake, Dianora, here is glorious news!
Ippolito, our foeman's only son,

Is caught red-handed on some midnight raid,
Taken with a rope-ladder 'neath his cloak,
Bound for some theft or felony, no doubt;
And as he offers neither excuse nor plea,
He is to suffer at the hour of noon,
In spite of his proud father's threats and cries.
All that the criminal asks by way of boon
Is he may pass our palace as he goes
Unto the scaffold.   A queer fancy that !
But all the better sport it makes for us,
And we need neither pity nor deny !
So rise, sweet sister, don your bravest gear,
For all the household on the balcony
Will sit to jeer the fellow as he wends,
And in the midst of us one Bardi Rose
Must be to grace and enjoy the spectacle,
The best that ever Florence saw ! "

                                                My boy,
Look not so startled !   Those were bitter days,
I said, and blood had flowed and hearts grown hard,
And hatred is contagious as disease.
Cosmo, my brother, was but as the rest.
He died at nine, ere ever thou wast born,
And I have paid for masses for his soul, —

For many, many masses have I paid ;
Heaven will not be hard with a babe like that,
The Frate tells me so, and I am sure.

What was I saying?   So I rose that day
A traitor unsuspected mid his foes,
Who were my friends, hiding 'neath feignèd smiles
A purpose desperate as was my hope.
I rose, and let them deck me as they would,
Put on my jewels, star my hair with pearls,
And all the while a voice like funeral dirge
Sang in my half-crazed ears, or seemed to sing,
The fragment and the cadence of a song.
" Ah, death, the end of grief, what do I care? "
Then I stood up among my tiring-maids,
And saw myself in the long Venice glass
A vision of pale splendor, as I moved
To take my station on the balcony,
In the mid place, the very front of all,
Set like a bride in festival array,
Among the laughing, chattering, peering throng,
To see the hated foeman of our race
Led past the palace on his way to die !
My love, my husband, my Ippolito,
Led past our palace on his way to die !

And up the stairs, and filled the palace full;
And high and low joined in an equal plea
That the long feud be stanched, and as a pledge
Of lasting peace we two be wedded straight.
But still my father frowned and closed his ears,
And still my brothers fumbled at their swords;
But when Count Buondelmonti, aged and gray,
And shattered with the horror just escaped
Suspense and heavy sickness, hurried in,
And kissed my hands, and knelt before my feet
And blessèd me, the savior of his son,
While with redoubled zeal the Podesta
Urged, and the noble lords, — Heaven touched the
    hearts, —
They gave consent; and so the feud was healed,
And the next day my Love and I were wed.

And twenty glad years came and fleetly sped,
Each like a separate rose which buds and falls
Duly and fragrantly and is not missed.
'T was then he carved as a memorial
On the façade of the old Sta. Maria
Sopr, Arno, " *Fuccio mi fecé*" and the date —
" I made myself a robber;" and he laughed,

And said I was the treasure that he stole ;
Ah me ! and then he sailed unto the wars,
And all the years that have gone by since then
Are as sad night shades steeped in deadly dews.
Death hath been busy with us, as thou knowest ;
Thou art the youngest of my six fair sons,
Thou art the only one to close my eyes
When time shall come and puzzles be explained.
How did the old song run ?   " My Rose is there."
If I shall wake in Paradise one day
And find him safe, and safely still my own,
Not won away from me by some new face,
And see his eyes with the old steadfast look,
Why, that will be enough, that will be heaven !
But if, instead, I find another there
Close to his side where once I used to rest,
No matter who it be, angel or saint,
I must cry " Shame !" whate'er the penalty.
God will not need to send me down to fires,
But only bid me stay in heaven and look !

HERE AND THERE.

E sit beside the lower feast to-day ;
    She at the higher.
Our voices falter as we bend to pray ;
    In the great choir
Of happy saints she sings, and does not tire.

We break the bread of patience, and the wine
    Of tears we share ;
She tastes the vintage of that glorious vine
    Whose branches fair
Set for the healing of all nations are.

I wonder is she sorry for our pain,
    Or if, grown wise,
She wondering smiles, and counts them idle, vain, —
    These heavy sighs,
These longings for her face and happy eyes.

Smile on, then, darling ! As God wills, is best.
        We loose our hold,
Content to leave thee to the deeper rest,
        The safer fold,
To joy's immortal youth while we grow old ;

Content the cold and wintry day to bear,
        The icy wave,
And know thee in immortal summer there,
        Beyond the grave ;
Content to give thee to the Love that gave.

FORWARD.

ET me stand still upon the height of life;
 Much has been won, though much there is to
  win.
I am a little weary of the strife;
 Let me stand still awhile, nor count it sin
To cool my hot brow, ease the travel pain,
And then address me to the road again.

Long was the way, and steep and hard the climb;
 Sore are my limbs, and fain I am to rest.
Behind me lie long sandy tracks of time;
 Before me rises the steep mountain crest.
Let me stand still; the journey is half done,
And when less weary I will travel on.

There is no standing still! Even as I pause,
 The steep path shifts and I slip back apace.

Movement was safety; by the journey-laws
   No help is given, no safe abiding-place,
No idling in the pathway hard and slow :
I must go forward, or must backward go !

I will go up then, though the limbs may tire,
   And though the path be doubtful and unseen ;
Better with the last effort to expire
   Than lose the toil and struggle that have been,
And have the morning strength, the upward strain,
The distance conquered, in the end made vain.

Ah, blessed law ! for rest is tempting sweet,
   And we would all lie down if so we might ;
And few would struggle on with bleeding feet,
   And few would ever gain the higher height,
Except for the stern law which bids us know
We must go forward or must backward go.

IN HER GARDEN.

TILL swings the scarlet pentstemon
　　Like threaded rubies on its stem,
　　　In the hid spot she loved so well;
Still bloom wild roses brave and fair,
And like a bubble borne in air
　　Floats the shy Mariposa's bell.

Like torches lit for carnival,
The fiery lilies, straight and tall,
　　Burn where the deepest shadow is;
Still dance the columbines cliff-hung,
And like a broidered veil outflung
　　The mazy-blossomed clematis.

Her garden!　All is silent now,
Save bell-note from some wandering cow,
　　Or rippling lark-song far away,
Or whisper from the wind-stirred leaves,

Or mourning dove which grieves and grieves,
   And " Lost ! lost ! lost ! " still seems to say.

Where is the genius of the place, —
The happy voice, the happy face,
   The feet whose light, unerring tread
Needed no guide in wildwood ways,
But trod the rough and tangled maze
   By natural instinct taught and led?

Upon the wind-blown mountain-spur
Chosen and loved as best by her,
   Watched over by near sun and star,
Encompassed by wide skies, she sleeps,
And not one jarring murmur creeps
   Up from the plain her rest to mar.

Sleep on, dear heart ! we would not break
Thy slumber for our sorrow's sake :
   The cup of life, with all its zest,
Thy ardent nature quaffed at full ;
Now, in the twilight long and cool,
   Take thou God's final gift of rest.

And still below the grape-vine swings;
The Mariposa's fragile wings
   Flutter, red lilies light their flame,
Larks float, the dove still plains and grieves;
But while one heart that loved thee lives,
   Still shall thy garden bear thy name.

ON EASTER DAY.

W E light the Easter fire, and the Easter lamps we
      trim,
    And lilies rear their chaliced cups in churches
      rich and dim,
And chapel low and Minster high the same triumphant
      strains
In city and in village raise, and on the lonely plains.

"Life" is the strain, and "endless life" the chiming bells
    repeat, —
A word of victory over death, a word of promise sweet;
And as the great good clasps the less, the sun a myriad
      rays,
So do a hundred thoughts of joy cling round our Easter
      days.

And one, which seems at times the best and dearest of
      them all,
Is this: that all the many dead in ages past recall,

With the friends who died so long ago that memory seeks
 in vain
To call the vanished faces back, and make them live again;

And those so lately gone from us that still they seem to be
Beside our path, beside our board, in viewless company, —
A light for all our weary hours, a glory by the way, —
All, all the dead, the near, the far, take part in Easter day!

They share the life we hope to share, as once they shared
 in this;
They hold in fast possession our heritage of bliss.
Theirs is the sure, near Presence toward which we reach
 and strain;
On Easter day, on Easter day, we all are one again.

Oh, fairest of the fair, high thoughts that light the Easter
 dawn !
Oh, sweet and true companionship which cannot be with-
 drawn !
" The Lord is risen ! " sealed lips repeat out of the
 shadows dim ;
" The Lord is risen," we answer back, " and all shall rise
 in him ! "

"DER ABEND IST DER BESTE."

THE morning hours are joyful fair,
    With call of bird and scent of dew;
    And blent with shining gold and blue
And glad the summer noontides are;
The slow sun lingering seeks the west,
    As loath to leave and grieve so soon
    The long and fragrant afternoon;
But still the evening is the best.

Day may be full as day may be, —
    Her hands all heaped with gifts, her eyes
    Alight with joyful prophecies;
But still we turn where wistfully
The veilèd evening, dimly fair,
    Stands in the shadow without speech,
    And holds her one gift out to each, —
Her gift of rest, for all to share.

Ah! sweetly falls the sunset glow
  On silver hairs, all peaceful bent.
  To catch the last rays, and content
To watch the twilight softly grow;
Content to face the night and keep
  The peaceful vigil of the eve,
  And like a little child to breathe
A "Now I lay me down to sleep."

Ah, close of life! Ah, close of day!
  Which thinks of morn without regret;
  Which thinks of busy noon, and yet
Grieves not to put its toils away;
Which, calmed with thoughts of coming rest,
  Watches the sweet, still evening fade,
  Counting its hours all unafraid, —
Surely the evening is the best.

OPTIMISM.

YOU tell me, with a little scorn,
    A pitying blame in look and touch,
Of conscious worldly-wisdom born,
    That I am hopeful over much;

That all my swans are veriest geese,
    My cheerfulness an easy vent
For animal spirits, and my peace
    A cheap, contemptible content;

That it is shallow to be glad,
    Idle to hope and vain to trust,
Because all good is mixed with bad,
    And men are liars, and flesh is dust;

That wisdom grimly prophesies,
    And sits distrustful and alert,
Peering with far, experienced eyes
    For what may cheat and what may hurt.

I do not know if you are right;
But these I hold as certainties:
That God made day as well as night,
And joy as well as pain is his;

That if philosophy means doubt,
And wisdom boding discontents,
Men may do better far without
These all-divine accomplishments!

That souls are stronger to endure
The heavy woes which all may taste,
If, holding to God's promise sure,
They wait his time, not making haste

To grieve, anticipating ill;
How shall they know what sweet, hid thing
He keeps in store for souls who still
Follow his beck unquestioning?

Joy is the lesson set for some,
For others pain best teacher is;
We know not which for us shall come,
But both are Heaven's high ministries.

OPTIMISM.

The swollen torrent rages high ;
   The path ahead is steep and wet.
What then ?   We still are safe and dry ;
   We need not cross that torrent yet !

Perhaps the waters may subside ;
   There may be paths which skirt the flood.
God holds our hand.   With him for guide
   We need not fear ; for he is good.

Meanwhile there is the sun, the sky,
   And life the joy, and love the zest ;
And, spite of scorn and pity, I
   Will taste to-day, and trust the rest.

"HE SHALL DRINK OF THE BROOK BY THE WAY."

THE way is hot, the way is long,
'T is weary hours to even-song,
    And we must travel though we tire;
But all the time beside the road
Trickle the small, clear rills of God,
    At hand for our desire.

Quick mercies, small amenities,
Brief moments of repose and ease, —
    We stoop, and drink, and so fare on,
Unpausing, but re-nerved in strength
From hour to hour, until at length
    Night falleth, and the day is done.

The birds sip of the wayside rill,
And raise their heads in praises, still
    Upborne upon their flashing wings;

So drinking thus along the way,
Our little meed of thanks we pay
   To Him who fills the water-springs,

And deals with equal tenderness
The larger mercies and the less :
   " O Lord, of good the fountain free,
Close by our hard day's journeying
Be thou the all-sufficing spring,
   And hourly let us drink of thee."

THREE PICTURES.

I.

LOVE AND DEATH.

UPON the threshold of his guarded home
        Stands Love the child.
    A thousand roses bloom above his head
With rain of dewy petals white and red ;
All fair and joyous things themselves array
To deck and soften for dear Love the way.
He stands where often he has stood before ;
But now his face is pale, his eyes all wild,
A strange and boding tread has caught his ear,
An awful, hovering shape sweeps into view,
And all his soul is rent with wrath and fear —
        What can Love do?

Poor Love ! brave Love ! he nerves his feeble arm,
        He grasps his bow ;
The dreadful guest has seized the rainbow wings.
In vain Love strives with tears and shudderings,

In vain he lifts appealing eyes of prayer;
There is no pity or relenting there.
No power has Love to deprecate or charm,
Vain are his puny wiles against this foe;
The roses wither in the icy breath
Which eddies the defenceless portals through,
And, brushing Love aside, in passes Death —
    What can Love do?

II.

LOVE AND LIFE.

THE way is steep, and hard to tread, and drear;
Piercing and bleak the icy atmosphere.
My feet are bruised and bleeding, and my eyes
Can only with dim questionings seek the skies.
How could I walk a step without thine aid?
How face the awful silence unafraid?
How bear the star-rays and the moon-glance cold?
    Loose not thine hold!

Earth and its kindly ways seem very far,
And yet the shining skies no nearer are;
Except for thee, dear Love, I could not go
Over the hard rocks, the untrodden snow

But had sat down content with lower things,
With scanty crumbs and waning water-springs, —
A wingèd thing whose wings might not unfold :
    Loose not thine hold !

Loose not thine hold ! let me feel all the while
The quickening impulse of thy tender smile
Luring me on, and catch, as if in trance,
The lovely reverence of thy downward glance,
The pity and the splendor of thy face,
The recognition like a soft embrace :
Until my feet shall tread the streets of gold,
    Loose not thy hold !

III.

PAOLO È FRANCESCA.

THE mighty blast which sweeps and girdles hell
Drives us before it, whither none may tell.
No pause, no goal, no time of respite, — well,
    We are together !

Circling forever in a dark abyss,
Linked by a fate as wild as passionless,
One only thing is left us, — it is this :
    We are together !

THE TWO SHORES.

UPON the river's brink I stand
  Beside the rushing water's flow,
  And look from off the shore I know,
The safe and dear familiar land,
Unto another shore, which lies
Mist-veiled beneath the crimsoning skies.
This is a shore, and that a shore.
Does the earth cease, to rise once more
    Beyond the river's span?
Ah no! the shores are clasped in one;
The same firm earth goes on, goes on,
Though hidden for a little space
    From eye or tread of man.

Upon another shore we stand
  Beside a darker water's flow,
  And catch beyond the earth we know

Faint glimpses of another land
Dreaming in sunshine, half descried
Beyond the rushing river-tide.
It is life here, and life is there :
We look from fair things to most fair,
    The river rolls between ;
But held and bound and clasped in one,
Immortal life goes on, goes on,
Though only from the farther strand
    The union can be seen.

"ARISE, SHINE, FOR THY LIGHT HAS COM

ONG time in sloth, long time in sin,
 Contented with thy dark estate
  Hast thou abode, O soul of mine ;
Now dawns the morning, fair though late,
 Her sunny tides are sweeping in.
  Thy light has come ; arise and shine !

The sheathèd bud which all night long
 Has folded close its purple up
  Upon the morning-glory vine ;
At the first rose-flush, the first song,
 Unrolls its petals, rears its cup,
  And, light being come, makes haste to shine.

It cannot clasp the whole bright day,
 Nor the wide-brimming sea of dew
  Within its curve exact and fine.

Of countless beams a single ray,
　　One little freshening sip or two,
　　　It takes, and so is glad to shine.

Make ready likewise, O my soul !
　　God's blessed day has dawned ; partake !
　　　Anoint thy head with oil and wine ;
From the great sum, the mighty whole,
　　Thy little crumb and portion break,
　　　And, giving thanks, arise and shine !

A WITHERED VIOLET.

 PLUCKED·a purple violet,
　　Its petals were all dewy wet,
　　I held it tightly for an hour,
And then I dropped the faded flower;
Dropped it and lost unconsciously,
Scarce thinking of the how or why.
'T was hours since, but my fingers yet
Are scented with the violet;
The fragrant spell, invisible,
Has caught and holds me in its sway.
I would not flee if flight might be;
The violet still rules my day.

I plucked a flower when life was young,
I chose it all the flowers among.
It was so fresh, it was so fair,
Heaven's very dew seemed cradled there;

A little while it smiled in morn,
And then it withered and was gone.
'T is long years since, but every hour
I taste the perfume of that flower.
Still it endures, and all day pours
A balm of fragrance on the way.
I catch its breath high over death ;
A memory still rules my day.

DARKENED.

IGH in the windy lighthouse tower
  The lamps are burning free,
  Each sending with good-will and power
    Its message o'er the sea,
Where ships are sailing out of sight,
Hidden in storm and cloud and night.

On the white waves that seethe and dash
  A ruddy gleam is shed ;
Above, the lighted windows flash
  Alternate gold and red,
Save where one sad and blinded glass
Forbids the happy light to pass.

The hungry sea entreats the light,
  The struggling light is fain,
But obdurate and blank as night
  Rises the darkened pane,
Casting a shadow long and black
Along the weltering ocean track.

Ah, who shall say what drowning eyes
　Yearn for that absent ray ;
What unseen fleets and argosies,
　Ploughing a doubtful way,
Seek through the night, and grope and strain
For guidance from that darkened pane?

Ah, Light Divine, so full, so free !
　Ah, world that lies in night !
Ah, guiding radiance ! shine through me
　Brightly and still more bright,
Nor ever be thy rays in vain
Because I am a " darkened pane."

THE KEYS OF GRANADA.

IS centuries since they were torn away,
    Those sad-faced Moors from their belovèd
       Spain;
In long procession to the wind-swept bay,
  With sobs and muttered curses, fierce with pain,
  They took their woful road and never came again.

Behind them lay the homes of their delight,
  The marble courtyards and cool palaces,
Where fountains flashed and shimmered day and night
  'Neath dusk and silver blooms of blossoming trees.
  They closed the echoing doors, and bore away the keys.

Palace and pleasure-garden are forgot;
  The marble walls have crumbled long ago;
Their site, their ownership, remembered not,
  And helpless wrath alike and hopeless woe
  Are cooled and comforted by Time's all-healing flow.

But still the children of those exiled Moors,
   A sad transplanted stem on alien shore,
Keep as their trust — and will while time endures —
   The rusty keys which their forefathers bore ;
   The keys of those shut doors which ne'er shall open
     more.

The doors are dust, but yet the hope lives on ;
   The walls are dust, but memories cannot die ;
And still each sad-faced father tells his son
   Of the lost homes, the blue Granadian sky,
   The glory and the wrong of those old days gone by.

Ah, keys invisible of happy doors
   Which long ago our own hands fastened tight !
We treasure them as do those hapless Moors,
   Though dust the palaces of our delight,
   Vacant and bodiless and vanished quite.

Keys of our dear, dead hopes, we prize them still,
   Wet them with tears, embalm with useless sighs ;
And at their sight and touch our pulses still
   Waken and throb, and under alien skies
   We taste the airs of home and gaze in long-closed eyes

BEREAVED.

WHEN Lazarus from his three days' tomb
   Fronted with dazzled eyes the day,
  And all the amazèd crowd made room,
As, wrapped in shroud, he went his way,
   His sisters daring scarce to touch
   His hand, their wonderment was such;

When friends and kindred met at meat,
   And in the midst the man just dead
Sat in his old-time wonted seat,
   And poured the wine, and shared the bread
With the old gesture that they knew, —
Were they all glad, those sisters two?

Did they not guess a hidden pain
   In the veiled eyes which shunned their gaze;
A dim reproach, a pale disdain
   For human joys and human ways;
A loneliness too deep for speech,
Which all their love might never reach?

And as the slowly ebbing days
   Went by, and Lazarus went and came
Still with the same estrangèd gaze,
   His loneliness and loss the same,
Did they not whisper as they grieved,
" We are consoled — and he bereaved " ?

Oh, weeper by a new-heaped mound,
   Who vexes Heaven with outcries vain,
That, if but for one short hour's round,
   Thy heart's desire might come again, —
The buried form, the vanished face,
The silent voice, the dear embrace, —

Think if he came, as Lazarus did,
   But came reluctant, with surprise,
And sat familiar things amid
   With a new distance in his eyes,
A distance death had failed to set, —
If hearts met not when bodies met !

If when you smiled you heard him sigh,
   And when you spoke he only heard
As men absorbed hear absently
   The idle chirping of a bird,

As, rapt in thoughts surpassing speech,
His mind moved on beyond your reach;

And still your joy was made his pain,
   And still the distance wider grew,
His daily loss your daily gain,
  · Himself become more strange to you
Than when your following soul sought his
In the vast secret distances ; —

If, death once tasted, life seemed vain
   To please or tempt or satisfy,
And all his longing was again
   To be released and free to die,
To get back to scarce-tasted bliss, —
What grief could be so sharp as this?

"HOW CAN THEY BEAR IT UP IN HEAVEN?"

HOW can they bear it up in heaven,
    They who so loved, and love us yet,
    If they can see us still, and know
The heavy hours that come and go,
    The fears that sting, the cares that fret,
The hopes belied, the helps ungiven?

Can they sit watching us all day,
    Measure our tears, and count our sighs,
And mark each throb and stab of pain,
The ungranted wish, the longing vain,
    And still smile on with happy eyes,
Content on golden harps to play?

Ah no! we will not do them wrong!
    When mothers hear their babies cry
For broken toy or trivial woe,
They smile, for all their love, — they know
    Laughter shall follow presently,
And sighing turn to merry song.

They are not cruel, that they smile ;
   Their eyes, grown old, can farther see,
Weighing the large thing and the less
With wise, experienced tenderness, —
   The moment's grief with joy to be
In such a little, little while.

Just so the angels, starry-eyed,
   With vision cleared and made all-wise,
Look past the storm-rack and the rain
And shifting mists of mortal pain
   To where the steadfast sunshine lies,
And everlasting summer-tide.

They see, beyond the pang, the strife,
   (To us how long, to them how brief !)
The compensation and the balm,
The victor's wreath, the conqueror's palm —
   They see the healing laid to grief,
They see unfold the perfect life.

For all our blind, impatient pain,
   Our desolate and sore estate,
They see the door that open is
Of Heaven's abundant treasuries,

The comforts and the cures that wait
The bow of promise in the rain.

And even as they watch, they smile,
    With eyes of love, as mothers may,
Nor grieve too much although we cry,
Because joy cometh presently,
    And sunshine, and the fair new day,
When we have wept a little while.

WAVE AFTER WAVE.

UT of the bosom of the sea,
From coasts where dim, rich treasures be,
By vast and urging forces blent,
Untired, untiring, and unspent,
The glad waves speed them one by one;
And, goal attained and errand done,
They lap the sands and softly lave, —
Wave after wave, wave after wave.

As stirred by longing for repose
Higher and higher each wave goes,
Striving to clasp with foam-white hands
The yielding and eluding sands;
And still the sea, relentless, grim,
Calls his wild truants back to him, —
Recalls the liberty he gave
Wave after wave, wave after wave.

All sad at heart and desolate
They heed the call, they bow to fate;

And outward swept, a baffled train,
Each feels his effort was in vain.
But fed by impulse lent by each
The gradual tide upon the beach
Rises to full, and thunders brave,
Wave after wave, wave after wave.

Ah, tired, discouraged heart and head,
Look up, and be thou comforted !
Thy puny effort may seem vain,
Wasted thy toil and naught thy pain,
Thy brief sun quench itself in shade,
Thy worthiest strength be weakness made,
Caught up in one great whelming grave,
Wave after wave, wave after wave.

Yet still, though baffled and denied,
Thy spended strength has swelled the tide.
A feather's weight where oceans roll —
One atom in a mighty whole —
God's hand uncounted agencies
Marshals and notes and counts as his :
His sands to bind, his threads to save,
His tides to build, wave after wave.

THE WORD WITH POWER.

OW shall the Word be preached with power?
    Not with elaborate care and toil,
    With wastings of the midnight oil,
With graceful gesture studied well,
And full intonèd syllable;
With trope and simile lending force
To subdivisions of discourse,
Or labored feeling framed to please —
The word of power is not in these.

How shall the Word be preached with power?
    Not by a separate holiness
    Which stands aloof to warn and bless,
Speaking as from a higher plane
Which common men may not attain;
Which treats of sin and want and strife
As things outside the priestly life,
And only draws anigh to chide,
Holding a saintly robe aside.

How shall the Word be preached with power?
  Ah, needless to debate and plan !
  Heart answereth unto heart in man ;
  Out of the very life of each
  Must come the power to heal or teach.
  The life all eloquent may grieve,
  The brain may subtly work and weave,
  But if the heart take not its share,
  The word of power is wanting there.

How shall the Word be preached with power?
  Go, preacher, search thy soul, and mark
  Each want, each weakness, every dark
  And painful dint where life and sin
  Have beaten their hard impress in :
  Apply the balm, and test the cure,
  And heal thyself, and be thou sure
  That which helps thee has power again
  To help the souls of other men.

How shall the Word be preached with power?
  Go ask the suffering and the poor,
  Go ask the beggar at thy door,

Go to the sacred page and read
What served the old-time want and need :
The clasping hand, the kindling eye,
Virtue given out unconsciously,
The self made selfless hour by hour, —
In these is preached the Word with power !

TO FELICIA SINGING.

HE sat where sunset shadows fell,
    And sunset rays, a miracle
        Of palest blue and rose and amber,
Touched her and folded in their spell.

Her golden head against the sky
Was traced and outlined tenderly,
    And, lily-soft in the soft late sunshine,
Her fair face blossomed to my eye.

She sang of love with tuneful breath,
Of sorrow, sweet as aught love saith;
    Of noble pain, immortal longing,
And hope which stronger is than death.

And every word and every tone
Seemed born of something all my own.
    'Twas I who sang, 'twas I who suffered;
Mine was the joyance, mine the moan.

Each lovely, vibrant, rapturous strain
Fulfilled my passion and my pain.
   I was the instrument she played on ;
I was her prelude and refrain.

And as dim echoes float and play
Through forests at the close of day,
   Farther and farther, breathed mysterious
From glades and copses far away,

So echoed through my heart her song,
Deeper and deeper borne along,
   Waking to life half-unsuspected
Grievings and hopes and yearnings strong.

Ah ! life and heart may weary be,
And youth may fail, and love may flee ;
   But when I hear her, see her singing,
The world grows beautiful to me.

EURYDICE.

HIS prayer availed!   Touched by the tuneful plea,
The Lord of Death relaxed his iron hold,
And out of the swart shadows, deep and cold,
Stole the lost wife, the fair Eurydice.
He felt her soft arms in the old embrace,
He guessed the smile upon her unseen face,
And joyful turned him from the dreadful place.

A little patience, and all had been well;
A little faith, and bale had changed to bliss:
Was it too much that he should ask for this,
Whose love had dared the steep descent of hell?
Had faced the Furies and the tongues of fire,
The reek of torment, rising high and higher,
Proserpina's sad woe and Pluto's ire?

It seemed a little thing to hope and ask
That the glad wife, just rescued from the dead,
Should go unquestioning where her Orpheus led.
But no; for woman's strength too hard the task.,
"Why dost thou turn thine eyes away from me?
Am I grown ugly, then, unfit to see?
Unkind!   Thou lovest not Eurydice!"

Was it because so short a time she stayed
Among the dead that she had not grown wise?
Do petty doubts and fears and jealousies,
Vanity, selfishness, the stain and shade
On mortal love, survive the poignant thrust
Which, winnowing souls from out their hindering dust,
Should wake the eyes to see, the heart to trust?

If we came back to those who love us so,
And fain would plead with Heaven for our recall,
Should we come back having forgotten all
The wisdom which all spirits needs must know?
Would the old faults revive, the old scars sting,
The old capacities for suffering
Quicken to life even in our quickening?

Oh, lovely myth, with just this marring stain!
I will not think that such deep wrong can be.
If ever it were given to one again
Earthward to turn in answer to Love's plea,
Surely 't would come in hushed and reverent guise,
With gentlest wisdom in far-seeing eyes,
Ripened for life by knowing Paradise.

THREE WORLDS.

ITHIN three worlds my Sorrow dwells ;
    Each made her own by heavenly right ;
    And one is sadly sweet and fair,
And one is bright beyond compare,
    And one is void of light.

One is the world of long-past things ;
    There she can go at will, and sit
And sun herself in love's embrace,
And see upon a vanished face
    The tender, old-time meanings flit.

The second, veiled in glory dim,
    She only dares in part explore ;
Upon its misty bound she stands,
And reaches out imploring hands
    And straining eyes, but does no more.

It is the world of unknown joy,
　Where thou, Beloved, amid thy kin,
The saints of God, the Sons of Light,
The company in robes of white,
　Hast been made free to enter in.

She sees thee, companied with these,
　Standing far off among the Blest,
And is content to watch and wait,
To stand afar without the gate,
　Nor interrupt thy perfect rest.

And so she turns, and down she sinks
　To her third world, that dreary one,
Which once was shared and lit by thee,
And never any more can be,
　In which she dwelleth all alone.

It were too dark a world to bear,
　Could she not go, her pain to still,
Into the fair world of the Past,
Into the glory, sure and vast,
　Made thine by the Eternal Will.

In these three worlds my Sorrow sits,
  And each is dear because of thee ;
I joyed in that, I wait in this,
And in the fulness of thy bliss
  Thou waitest too, I know. for me.

OPPORTUNITY.

BUT yesterday, but yesterday,
  She stood beside our dusty way,
  Outreaching for one moment's space
The key to fortune's hiding-place.

With wistful meanings in her eyes,
Her radiance veiled in dull disguise,
A moment paused, then turned and fled,
Bearing her message still unsaid.

And we? Our eyes were on the dust;
Still faring on as fare all must
In the hot glare of midday sun
Until the weary way be done.

So, fast and far she sped and flew
Into the depths of ether blue;
And we, too late, make bitter cry,
" Come back, dear Opportunity ! "

In vain : the fleet, unpausing wings
Stay not in their bright journeyings ;
And sadly sweet as funeral bell
The answer drops, " Farewell ! Farewell ! "

CHRIST BEFORE PILATE.

A PICTURE.

 DIM rich space, a vault of arching gold,
    A furious, shouting rabble pressing near,
A single sentinel to bar and hold
      With his one spear.

I see the Roman ruler careless sit
    To judge the cause in his accustomed place ;
I see the coarse, dull, cruel meanings flit
      Across his face.

I see the pitiless priests who urge and rave,
    Intent to see the victim sacrificed,
Fearful that scruple or that plea should save —
      Where is the Christ?

Not that pale shape which stands amid the press,
    In gentle patience uncomplainingly,
Clad in the whiteness of his Teacher's dress —
      That is not he !

That slender flame were easily blown out ;
   One furious gust of human hate, but one !
One chilling breath of treason or of doubt —
      And it were gone !

But thou, O mighty Christ, endurest still ;
   Quenchless thy fire, fed by immortal breath,
Lord of the heart, Lord of the erring will,
      And Lord of Death !

King of the world, thou livest to the end,
   Ruling the nations as no other can ;
Best comrade, healer, teacher, guide, best friend
      And help of man.

I see thee, not a wan and grieving shape,
   Facing, like lamb led forth for sacrifice,
The destiny from which is no escape,
      With mild, sad eyes, —

But strong and brave and resolute to bear,
   Knowing that Death, once conquered, was to be
Thy willing thrall, thy servant grave and fair,
      Best help to thee !

The vision changes on the pictured scene ;
  The pallid Victim fades, and in his place
Comes a victorious, steadfast, glorious mien,
  The true Christ's face.

NON OMNIS MORIAR.

H, blue and glad the summer skies,
And golden green the widths of plain
Where sun and shadow mingled lay,
As forth we went, with gay intent,
Across the Mesa's flowery rise,
To where the shimmering mountain chain
Beckoned and shone from far away !

The noontide flashed, the noontide sang,
Along the glittering distant track ;
The dancing wind made answer brave.
It seemed that all kept festival,
That joy fires burned and joy bells rang ;
But still our hearts went hovering back
To sit beside one lonely grave.

It seems so strange, so half unkind,
That still the earth with life should stir,
That still we smile, and still we jest,

NON OMNIS MORIAR.

And drink our share of sun and air
And joy — and leave her there behind;
   Nor share such happy things with her
    Who always gave us all her best!

And yet — our love is loyal still;
   And yet — she joyed to have us gay;
    And yet — the moving world moves on,
And does not wait our sad estate,
To soothe our hurt or note our ill,
   But, touch by touch, and day by day,
    Heals us, and changes every one.

But she?   What is her work to do?
   For never tell me that she lies
    Inactive, lifeless, in the mould,
Content to keep a moveless sleep
While worlds revolve in courses new.
   Her fiery zeal, her quick emprise,
    Could never brook such rest to hold!

That grave but hides her worn-out dress, —
   One of God's sure-winged messengers
    I see her, on swift errand sped,

Glad of the task which strong souls ask,
Earth's sharpest pain grown littleness
　　In the new tide of life made hers,
　　　　Smiling that we should call her dead !

Smile on, dear Heart, until the dawn !
　　When once the eternal heights are bared,
　　　And the long earthly shadows flit,
And with clear eyes we front the skies,
We too shall smile with heavenly scorn
　　At the dull, human selves who dared
　　　To call life " Death " and pity it !

AT DAWN OF DAY.

THE yellow lighthouse star is quenched
　　Across the lonely sea ;
　The mountains rend their misty veils,
　　The wind of dawn blows free ;
The waves beat with a gladder thrill,
　　Pulsing in lines of spray,
And fast and far chime on the bar —
　　God bless my Dear to-day !

A thousand leagues may lie between
　　A world of distance dim ;
But speeding with the speeding light
　　My heart goes forth to him.
Faster than wind or wave it flies,
　　As love and longing may,
And undenied stands by his side —
　　God bless my Dear to-day !

God bless him if he wake to smiles,
  Or if he wake to sighs ;
Temper his will to bear all fate,
  And keep him true and wise ;
Be to him all I fain would be
  Who am so far away, —
Light, counsel, consolation, cheer —
  God bless my Dear to-day !

The gradual light has grown full fain,
  And streameth far abroad.
The urgence of my voiceless plea
  Is gathered up by God.
Take some sweet thing which else were mine,
  Inly I dare to pray,
And with it brim his cup of joy —
  God bless my Dear to-day !

WHAT MIGHT HAVE BEEN.

O many things there might have been,
   Had our dear child not died.
  We count them up and call them o'er,
We weigh the less against the more, —
The joy she never knew or shared,
The bitter woes forever spared,
   The dangers turned aside,
Heaven's full security, — and then
Perplexed we sigh, — all might have been.

We might have seen her sweet cheeks glow
   With love's own happy bloom,
Her eyes with maiden gladness full,
Finding the whole world beautiful ;
We might have seen the joyance fail,
The dear face sadden and grow pale,
   The smiles fade into gloom,
Love's sun grow dim and sink again, —
Either of these it might have been.

We might have seen her with the crown
  Of wifehood on her head,
A queen of home's fair sovereignties,
With little children at her knees;
Or, broken-hearted and alone,
Bereft and widowed of her own,
  Mourning beside her dead, —
This thing or that, beyond our ken,
It might have been, it might have been.

There is no need of question now,
  No doubts or risks or fears :
Safe folded in the Eternal care,
Grown fairer each day and more fair,
With radiance in the clear young eyes
Which in cool depths of Paradise
  Look without stain of tears,
Reading the Lord's intent, and then
Smiling to think what might have been.

We too will smile, O dearest child !
  Our dull souls may not know
The deep things hidden from mortal sense,
Which feed thy heavenly confidence.

On this one sure thought can we rest,
That God has chosen for thee the best,
   Or else it were not so ;
He called thee back to Heaven again
Because he knew what might have been.

SOME TIME.

THE night will round into the morn,
     The angry storm-wind cease to beat,
    The spent bird preen his wet tired wing,
Grief ceaseth when the babe is born.
    There comes an end to hardest thing
        Some time, —
    Some time, some far time, late but sweet.

I could not keep on with the fight;
    I could not face my want, my sin,
    The baffled hope, the urgent foe,
The mighty wrong, the struggling right,
    Excepting that I surely know
        Some time —
    Some time, some dear time, — I shall win.

I could not hold so sure, so fast,
    The truth which is to me so true,
    The truth which men deride and shun,

Were I not sure it shall at last
  Be held as truth by every one
    Some time, —
    Some time all men shall own it too.

Some time the morning bells shall chime,
    Some time be heard the victor-song,
  Some time the hard goal be attained,
The puzzles shall be clear some time,
    The tears all shed, the gains all gained,
      Some time —
    Ah, dear time, tarry not too long !

THE STARS ARE IN THE SKY ALL DAY.

THE stars are in the sky all day;
　　Each linkèd coil of Milky Way,
　　And every planet that we know,
Behind the sun are circling slow.
They sweep, they climb with stately tread, —
Venus the fair and Mars the red,
Saturn engirdled with clear light,
And Jupiter with moons of white.
Each knows his path and keeps due tryst;
Not even the smallest star is missed
From those wide fields of deeper sky
Which gleam and flash mysteriously,
As if God's outstretched fingers must
Have sown them thick with diamond dust.
There are they all day long; but we,
Sun-blinded, have no eyes to see.

The stars are in the sky all day;
But when the sun has gone away,
And hovering shadows cool the west,
And call the sleepy birds to rest,
And heaven grows softly dim and dun,
Into its darkness one by one
Steal forth those starry shapes all fair —
We say steal forth, but they were there,
There all day long, unseen, unguessed,
Climbing the sky from east to west.
The angels saw them where they hid,
And so, perhaps, the eagles did,
For they can face the sharp sun-ray,
Nor wink, nor need to look away;
But we, blind mortals, gazed from far,
And did not see a single star.

I wonder if the world is full
Of other secrets beautiful,
As little guessed, as hard to see,
As this sweet starry mystery?
Do angels veil themselves in space,
And make the sun their hiding-place?
Do white wings flash as spirits go
On heavenly errands to and fro,

While we, down-looking, never guess
How near our lives they crowd and press?
If so, at life's set we may see
Into the dusk steal noiselessly
Sweet faces that we used to know,
Dear eyes like stars that softly glow,
Dear hands stretched out to point the way,
And deem the night more fair than day.

NOW.

LOVE me now! Love has such a little minute!
   Day crowds on day with swift and noiseless
      tread,
Life's end comes ere fairly we begin it;
   Pain jostles joy, and hope gives place to dread.
         Love me now!
It will be too late when we are dead!

Love me now! While we still are young together,
   While glad and brave the sun shines overhead,
Hand locked in hand, in blue, smiling weather.
   Sighing were sin, and variance ill bestead;
   It will be too late when you are dead!

Love me now! Shadows hover in the distance,
   Cold winds are coming, green leaves must turn red.
Frownest thou, my Love, at this sad insistence?
   Even this moment may the dart be sped.
         Love me now!
It will be too late when I am dead!

JUST BEYOND.

HEN out of the body the soul is sent,
　　As a bird speeds forth from the opened tent,
　　As the smoke flies out when it finds a vent,
　　　To lose itself in the spending, —

Does it travel wide, does it travel far,
To find the place where all spirits are?
Does it measure long leagues from star to star,
　　And feel its travel unending?

And caught by each baffling, blowing wind,
Storm-tossed and beaten, before, behind,
Till the courage fails and the sight is blind,
　　Must it go in search of its heaven?

I do not think that it can be so ;
For weary is life, as all men know,
And battling and struggling to and fro
　　Man goes from his morn to his even.

And surely this is enough to bear, —
The long day's work in the sun's hot glare,
The doubt and the loss which breed despair,
   The anguish of baffled hoping.

And when the end of it all has come,
And the soul has won the right to its home,
I do not believe it must wander and roam
   Through the infinite spaces groping.

No ; wild may the storm be, and dark the day,
And the shuddering soul may clasp its clay,
Afraid to go and unwilling to stay ;
   But when it girds it for going,

With a rapture of sudden consciousness,
I think it awakes to a knowledge of this,
That heaven earth's closest neighbor is,
   And only waits for our knowing ;

That 't is but a step from dark to day,
From the worn-out tent and the burial clay,
To the rapture of youth renewed for aye,
   And the smile of the saints uprisen ;

And that just where the soul, perplexed and awed,
Begins its journey, it meets the Lord,
And finds that heaven and the great reward
' Lay just outside of its prison !

CONTACT.

N O soul can be quite separate,
However set apart by fate,
However cold or dull or shy,
Or shrinking from the public eye.
The world is common to the race,
And nowhere is a hiding-place ;
Before, behind, on either side,
The surging masses press, divide ;
Behind, before, with rhythmic beat,
Is heard the tread of marching feet ;
To left, to right, they urge, they fare,
And touch us here, and touch us there.
Hold back your garment as you will,
The crowding world will rub it still.
Then, since such contact needs must be,
What shall it do for you and me?

Shall it be cold and hard alone,
As when a stone doth touch a stone,

Fruitless, unwelcome, and unmeant,
Put by as a dull accident,
While we pass onward, deaf and blind,
With no relenting look behind?
Or as when two round drops of rain,
Let fall upon a window-pane,
Wander, divergent, from their course,
Led by some blind, instinctive force,
Mingle and blend and interfuse,
Their separate shapes and being lose,
Made one thereafter and the same,
Identical in end and aim,
Nor brighter gleam, nor faster run,
Because they are not two, but one?

Or shall we meet in warring mood,
The contact of the fire and flood,
Decreed by Nature and by Will,
The one to warm, the one to chill,
The one to burn, the one to slake,
To thwart and counteract and make
Each other's wretchedness, and dwell
In hate irreconcilable?
Or as when fierce fire meets frail straw,

CONTACT.

And carries out the fatal law
Which makes the weaker thing to be
The prey of strength and tyranny ;
A careless touch, half scorn, half mirth,
A brief resistance, little worth ;
A little blaze soon quenched and marred,
And ashes ever afterward ?

No ; let us meet, since meet we must,
Not shaking off the common dust,
As if we feared our fellow-men,
And fain would walk aloof from them ;
Not fruitlessly, as rain meets rain,
To lose ourselves and nothing gain ;
Not fiercely, prey to adverse fate,
And not to spoil and desolate.
But as we meet and touch, each day,
The many travellers on our way,
Let every such brief contact be
A glorious, helpful ministry ;
The contact of the soil and seed,
Each giving to the other's need,
Each helping on the other's best,
And blessing, each, as well as blest.

AN EASTER SONG.

E bore to see the summer go ;
   We bore to see the ruthless wind
Beat all the golden leaves and red
In drifting masses to and fro,
   Till not a leaf remained behind ;
We faced the winter's frown, and said,
   "There comes reward for all our pain,
   For every loss there comes a gain ;
And spring, which never failed us yet,
   Out of the snow-drift and the ice
Shall some day bring the violet."

We bore — what could we do but bear ? —
   To see youth perish in its prime,
And hope grow faint, and joyance grieved,
And dreams all vanish in thin air,
   And beauty, at the touch of time,

AN EASTER SONG.

Become a memory, half believed ;
   Still we could smile, and still we said,
   " Hope, joy, and beauty are not dead ;
God's angel guards them all and sees —
   Close by the grave he sits and waits —
There comes a spring for even these."

We bore to see dear faces pale,
   Dear voices falter, smiles grow wan,
And life ebb like a tide at sea,
Till underneath the misty veil
   Our best belovèd, one by one,
Vanished and parted silently.
   We stayed without, but still could say,
   " Grief's winter dureth not alway ;
Who sleep in Christ with Christ shall rise.
   We wait our Easter morn in tears,
They in the smile of Paradise."

O thought of healing, word of strength l
   O light to lighten darkest way !
O saving help and balm of ill !
For all our dead shall dawn at length
   A slowly broadening Easter Day,
A Resurrection calm and still.

The little sleep will not seem long,
   The silence shall break out in song,
The sealèd eyes shall ope, — and then
   We who have waited patiently
Shall live and have our own again.

CONCORD.

MAY 31, 1882.

" FARTHER horizons every year ! "
  Oh, tossing pines which surge and wave
  Above the poet's just made grave,
And waken for his sleeping ear
The music that he loved to hear,
Through summer's sun and winter's chill,
With purpose stanch and dauntless will,
Sped by a noble discontent,
You climb toward the blue firmament, —
Climb as the winds climb, mounting high
The viewless ladders of the sky ;
Spurning our lower atmosphere,
Heavy with sighs and dense with night,
And urging upward year by year
To ampler air, diviner light.

" Farther horizons every year ! "
Beneath you pass the tribes of men,
Your gracious boughs o'ershadow them ;
You hear, but do not seem to heed

Their jarring speech, their faulty creed.
Your roots are firmly set in soil
Won from their humming paths of toil ;
Content their lives to watch and share,
To serve them, shelter, and upbear,
Yet bent to win an upward way
And larger gift of heaven than they,
Benignant view and attitude,
Close knowledge of celestial sign,
Still working for all earthly good
While pressing on to the Divine.

" Farther horizons every year ! "
So he, by reverent hands just laid
Beneath your boughs of wavering shade,
Climbed as you climb the upward way,
Knowing not boundary or stay.
His eyes surcharged with heavenly lights,
His senses steeped in heavenly sights,
His soul attuned to heavenly keys,
How should he pause for rest and ease,
Or turn his wingèd feet again,
To share the common feasts of men ?
He blessed them with his word and smile,

CONCORD.

But still, above their fickle moods,
Wooing, constraining him awhile,
Beckoned the shining altitudes.

" Farther horizons every year ! "
To what immeasurable height,
What clear irradiance of light,
What far and all-transcendent goal
Hast thou now risen, O steadfast soul !
We may not follow with our eyes
To where thy farther pathway lies,
Nor guess what vision vast and free
God keeps in store for souls like thee.
But still the pines that bend and wave
Their boughs above thy honored grave
Shall be thy emblem brave and fit,
Firm-rooted in the stalwart sod,
Blessing the earth while spurning it,
Content with nothing short of God.

HEREAFTER.

WHEN we are dead, when you and I are dead,
　　Have rent and tossed aside each earthly fetter,
　　And wiped the grave-dust from our wondering
　　　　eyes,
And stand together, fronting the sunrise,
　　I think that we shall know each other better.

Puzzle and pain will lie behind us then ;
　　All will be known and all will be forgiven.
We shall be glad of every hardness past,
And not one earthly shadow shall be cast
　　To dim the brightness of the bright new heaven.

And I shall know, and you as well as I,
　　What was the hindering thing our whole lives through,
Which kept me always shy, constrained, distressed ;
Why I, to whom you were the first and best,
　　Could never, never be my best with you ;

Why, loving you as dearly as I did,
    And prizing you above all earthly good,
I yet was cold and dull when you were by,
And faltered in my speech or shunned your eye,
    Unable quite to say the thing I would;

Could never front you with the happy ease
    Of those whose perfect trust has cast out fear,
Or take, content, from Love his daily dole.
But longed to grasp and be and have the whole,
    As blind men long to see, the deaf to hear.

My dear Love, when I forward look, and think
    Of all these baffling barriers swept away,
Against which I have beat so long and strained,
Of all the puzzles of the past explained,
    I almost wish that we could die to-day.

OUR DAILY BREAD.

"GIVE us our daily bread," we pray,
    And know but half of what we say.

The bread on which our bodies feed
Is but the moiety of our need.

The soul, the heart, must nourished be,
And share the daily urgency.

And though it may be bitter bread
On which these nobler parts are fed,

No less we crave the daily dole,
O Lord, of body and of soul !

Sweet loaves, the wine-must all afoam,
The manna, and the honey-comb, —

All these are good, but better still
The food which checks and moulds the will.

The sting for pride, the smart for sin,
The purging draught for self within,

The sorrows which we shuddering meet,
Not knowing their after-taste of sweet, —

All these we ask for when we pray,
" Give us our daily bread this day."

Lord, leave us not athirst, unfed ;
Give us this best and hardest bread,

Until, these mortal needs all past,
We sit at thy full feast at last,

The bread of angels broken by thee,
The wine of joy poured constantly.

SLEEPING AND WAKING.

OD giveth his beloved sleep;
   They lie securely 'neath his wing
   Till the night pale, the dawning break;
  Safe in its overshadowing
  They fear no dark and harmful thing; —
What does he give to those who wake?

To those who sleep he gives good dreams;
   For bodies overtasked and spent
Comes rest to comfort every ache;
   To weary eyes new light is sent,
   To weary spirits new content; —
What does God give to those who wake?

His angels sit beside the beds
   Of such as rest beneath his care.
Unweariedly their post they take,
   They wave their wings to fan the air,
   They cool the brow and stroke the hair, —
God comes himself to those who wake.

SLEEPING AND WAKING.

To fevered eyes that cannot close,
　To hearts o'erburdened with their lot,
He comes to soothe, to heal, to slake ;
　Close to the pillows hard and hot
　He stands, although they see him not,
And taketh care of those who wake.

Nor saint nor angel will he trust
　With this one blessed ministry,
Lest they should falter or mistake ;
　They guard the sleepers faithfully
　Who are the Lord's beloved ; but he
Watches by those beloved who wake.

Oh, in the midnight dense and drear,
　When life drifts outward with the tide,
And mortal terrors overtake,
　In this sure thought let us abide,
　And unafraid be satisfied, —
God comes himself to those who wake !

THORNS.

ROSES have thorns, and love is thorny too ;
 And this is love's sharp thorn which guards
  its flower,
That our beloved have the cruel power
To hurt us deeper than all others do.

The heart attuned to our heart like a charm,
 Beat answering beat, as echo answers song,
 If the throb falter, or the pulse beat wrong,
How shall it fail to grieve us or to harm?

The taunt which, uttered by a stranger's lips,
 Scarce heard, scarce minded, passed us like the wind,
 Breathed by a dear voice, which has grown unkind,
Turns sweet to bitter, sunshine to eclipse.

The instinct of a change we cannot prove,
 The pitiful tenderness, the sad too-much,
 The sad too-little, shown in look or touch, —
All these are wounding thorns of thorny love.

Ah, sweetest rose which earthly gardens bear,
   Fought for, desired, life's guerdon and life's end,
   Although your thorns may slay and wound and rend,
Still men must snatch you ; for you are so fair.

A NEW-ENGLAND LADY.

HE talks of " gentry " still, and " birth,"
    And holds the good old-fashioned creed
    Of widely differing ranks and station;
And gentle blood, whose obligation
    Is courteous word and friendly deed.

She knows her own ancestral line,
    And numbers all its links of honor ;
But in her theory of right living
Good birth involves good will, good giving, —
    A daily duty laid upon her.

Her hands are versed in household arts :
    She kneads and stirs, compounds and spices ;
Her bread is famous in the region ;
Her cakes and puddings form a legion
    Of sure successes, swift surprises.

A NEW-ENGLAND LADY.

A lady in her kitchen apron ;
   Always a lady, though she labors ;
She has a " faculty " prompt and certain,
Which makes each flower-bed, gown, and cur
   A standing wonder to her neighbors.

Her days seem measured by some planet
   More liberal than our common sun is ;
For she finds time when others miss it
The poor to cheer, the sick to visit,
   And carry brightness in where none is.

Behold her as, her day's work over,
   Her house from attic to door-scraper
In order, all her tasks completed,
She sits down, calm, composed, unheated,
   To read her Emerson or her paper.

She hears the new æsthetic Gospel,
   And unconvinced although surprised is ;
Her family knows what is proper.
She smiles, and does not care a copper,
   Although her carpet stigmatized is.

She does not quite accept tradition ;
    She has her private theory ready ;
Her shrewd, quaint insight baffles leading ;
And straight through dogma's special pleading
    She holds her own, composed and steady.

Kindness her law ; her king is duty.
    You cannot bend her though you break her ;
As tough as yew and as elastic
Her fibre ; unconvinced, unplastic, —
    She clasps conviction like a Quaker.

Long live her type, to be our anchor
    When times go wrong and true men rally,
Till aged Chocorua fails and bleaches
Beside the shining Saco reaches,
    Monadnock by the Jaffrey valley.

UNDER THE SNOW.

NDER the snow lie sweet things out of sight,
  Couching like birds beneath a downy breast ·
They cluster 'neath the coverlet warm and white,
And bide the winter-time in hopeful rest.

There are the hyacinths, holding ivory tips
  Pointed and ready for a hint of sun ;
And hooded violets, with dim, fragrant lips
  Asleep and dreaming fairy dreams each one.

There lurk a myriad quick and linkèd roots,
  Coiled for a spring when the ripe time is near ;
The brave chrysanthemum's pale yellow shoots
  And daffodils, the vanguard of the year ;

The nodding snowdrop and the columbine ;
  The hardy crocus, prompt to hear a call ;
Pensile wistaria and thick woodbine ;
  And valley lilies, sweetest of them all.

All undismayed, although the drifts are deep,
    All sure of spring and strong of cheer they lie ;
And we, who see but snows, we smile and keep
    The selfsame courage in the by and by.

Ah ! the same drifts shroud other precious things, —
    Flower-like faces, pallid now and chill,
Feet laid to rest after long journeyings,
    And fair and folded hands forever still.

All undismayed, in deep and hushed repose,
    Waiting a sweeter, further spring, they lie ;
And we, whose yearning eyes see but the snows,
    Shall we not trust, like them, the by and by?

SONNET

FOR A BIRTHDAY.

 WISH thee sound health and true sanity,
Ripe youth, a summer heart in age's snow,
Abiding joy in knowledge, wealth enow
That of the best thou ne'er mayst hindered be ;
Long life, love, marriage, children, faithful friends,
Purpose in all thy doing, stintless zeal,
Ambition, enthusiasm, the power to feel
Thy country dearer than thy private ends ;
The threefold joy of Nature, books, and fun,
To be thy solace in adversity,
To keep thy father's name as clean as he,
And so transmit it stainless to thy son ;
And lastly, crown of glory and of strife,
May honored death give thee Eternal Life.

Now count my wishes, and, the numbering done,
You 'll find the enumeration — twenty-one.

"MANY WATERS CANNOT QUENCH LOVE."

 LITTLE grave in a desolate spot,
   Where the sun scarce shines and flowers grow
      not,
  Where the prayers of the church are never heard,
And the funeral bell swings not in air,
  And the brooding silence is only stirred
By the cries of wild birds nesting there ;
  A low headstone, and a legend, green
  With moss : " Leonora, just seventeen."

Here she was laid long years ago,
A child in years, but a woman in woe.
  Her sorrowful story is half forgot,
Her playmates are old and bent and gray,
  And no one comes to visit the spot
Where, watched by the law, was hurried away
  The youth cut short, and the hapless bloom
  Which fled from its sorrow to find the tomb.

Her mourning kindred pleaded in vain
The broken heart and the frenzied brain ;
   The church had no pardon for such as died
Unblessed by the church, and sternly barred
   All holy ground to the suicide ;
So death as life to the girl was hard,
   And the potter's field with its deep disgrace
   Was her only permitted resting-place.

So the friends who loved her laid her there
With no word of comfort, no word of prayer,
   And years went by ; but as, one by one,
They dropped from their daily tasks and died,
   And turned their faces from the sun,
They were carried and buried by her side, —
   Each gave command that such should be,
   " For love to keep her company."

So the little grave, with the letters green,
Of " Leonora, just seventeen,"
   Is ringed about with kindred dust,
Not lonely like the other graves
   In that sad place, wherein are thrust
Outcasts and nameless folk and slaves,
   But gently held and folded fast
   In the arms that loved her first and last

O potter's field, did I call you bare?
No garden on earth can be more fair !
   For deathless love has a deathless bloom,
And the lily of faithfulness a flower,
   And they grow beside each lowly tomb,
And balm it with fragrance every hour ;
      And with God, who forgiveth till seven times seven,
      A potter's field may be gate of heaven.

UNEXHAUSTED.

ARE all the songs sung, all the music played?
   Are the keys quite worn out, and soundless
      quite,
Which since sweet fancy's dawning day have made
  Perpetual melody for man's delight,
  And charmed the dull day and the heavy night?

Must we go on with stale, repeated themes,
  Content with threadbare chords that faint and fail,
Till all the fairy fabric of old dreams
  Becomes a jaded, oft-repeated tale,
  And poetry grows tired, and romance pale?

I cannot think it; for the soul of man
  Is strung to answer to such myriad keys
Set and attuned and chorded on a plan
  Of intricate and vibrant harmonies,
  How shall we limit that, or measure these?

As free and urgent as the air that moves,
　As quick to tremble as Æolian strings,
The soul responds and thrills to hates and loves,
　Desires and hopes, and joys and sufferings,
　And sympathy's soft touch and anger's stings.

How dare we say the breezes all are blown,
　The chords have no reserved sweet in store ;
Or claim that all is tested and made known, —
　That nightingales may trill, or skylarks soar,
　But neither can surprise us any more ?

The world we call so old, God names his new ;
　The thought we christen stale shall outlast men,
While moons shall haunt the sky, and stars gleam through,
　While roses blossom on their thorny stem,
　And spring comes back again, and yet again ;

While human things like blossoms small and white
　Are dropped on earth from unseen parent skies,
The olden dreams shall please, the songs delight,
　And those who shape and weave fair fantasies
　Shall catch the answering shine in new-born eyes.

WELCOME AND FAREWELL.

WHEN the New Year came, we said,
   Half with hope and half with dread :
   " Welcome, child, new-born to be
Last of Time's great family !
All thy brethren, bent and gray,
Aged and worn, have passed away
To the place where dead years go, —
Place which mortals cannot know.
Thou art fairest of them all,
Ivory-limbed and strong and tall,
Gold hair blown back, and deep eyes
Full of happy prophecies ;
Rose-bloom on thy youthful cheek.
   Welcome, child ! "   And all the while
The sweet New Year did not speak,
   Though we thought we saw him smile.

When the Old Year went, we said,
Looking at his grim gray head,
At the shoulders burden-bowed,
And the sad eyes dark with cloud :

" Was he ever young and fair?
Did we praise his sunny hair
And glad eyes, with promise lit?
We can scarce remember it.
Treacherously he smiled, nor spoke,
Hiding 'neath his rainbow cloak
Store of grievous things to strew
On the way that we must go.
Vain to chide him ; old and weak,
　　He is dying ; let him die."
And the Old Year did not speak,
　　But we thought we heard him sigh.

LIFE.

ORE life we thirst for, but how can we take?
    We sit like children by the surging sea,
    Dip with our shallow shells all day, and make
A boast of the scant measure, two or three
Brief drops caught from the immensity;
But what are these the long day's thirst to slake?

There is the sea, which would not be less full,
    Though all the lands should borrow of its flood;
The sea of Life, fed by the beautiful
    Abounding river of the smile of God,
Source of supply and fountain of all good,
    Boundless and free and inexhaustible.

There is the sea; and close by is our thirst,
    Yet here we sit and gaze the waters o'er,
And dip our shallow shells in as at first,
    Just where the ripples break to wash the shore,
And catch a tantalizing drop, nor durst
    The depth or distance of the wave explore.

Ah, mighty ocean which we sport beside,
　Onè day thy wave will rise and foam, and we,
Lost in its strong, outgoing, refluent tide,
　Shall be swept out into the deeper sea,
Shall drink the life of life, and satisfied
　Smile at the shore from far eternity.

SHŬT IN.

And the Lord shut him in. — *Gen.* vii. 16.

AS it the Lord who shut me in
    Between these walls of pain?
  Who drew between me and the sun
The darkening curtains, one by one,
    Cold storm and bitter rain,
Hiding all happy things and fair,
  The flying birds, the blowing air,
    And bidding me to lie,
All sick of heart and faint and blind,
Waiting his will to loose or bind,
    To give or to deny?

Was it the Lord who shut me in
  Within this place of doubt?
I chose not doubt, my doubt chose me,
Not unpermitted, Lord, of thee, —
    It had not dared without :
What doubt shall venture to uprear
And whisper in a human ear,

If thou, Lord, dost forbid?
Yet is it of thy blessed will
That I sit questioning, grieving, chill,
  Nor joy as once I did?

Is it the Lord that shuts me in?
  Then I can bear to wait !
No place so dark, no place so poor,
So strong and fast no prisoning door,
  Though walled by grievous fate,
But out of it goes fair and broad
An unseen pathway, straight to God,
  By which I mount to thee.
When the same Love that shut the door
Shall lift the heavy bar once more,
  And set the prisoner free.

GOOD-BY.

THE interlacing verdurous screen
Of the stanch woodbine still is green,
And thickly set with milk-white blooms
Gold-anthered, breathing out perfumes;
The clematis on trellis bars
Still flaunts with white and purple stars;
No missing leaf has thinner made
The obelisks of maple shade;
Fresh beech boughs flutter in the breeze
Which, warm as summer, stirs the trees;
The sun is clear, the skies are blue:
But still a sadness filters through
The beauty and the bloom; and we,
Touched by some mournful prophecy,
Whisper each day: " Delay, delay!
Make not such haste to fly away!"
And they, with silent lips, reply:
" Summer is gone; we may not stay.
Summer is gone. Good-by! good-by!"

Roses may be as fragrant fair
As in the sweet June days they were ;
No hint of frost may daunt as yet
The clustering brown mignonette,
Nor chilly wind forbid to ope
The odorous, fragile heliotrope ;
The sun may be as warm as May,
The night forbear to chase the day,
And hushed in false security
All the sweet realm of Nature be :
But the South-loving birds have fled,
By their mysterious instinct led ;
The butterflies their nests have spun,
And donned their silken shrouds each one ;
The bees have hived them fast, while we
Whisper each day : " Delay, delay !
Make not such haste to fly away ! "
And all, with pitying looks, reply :
" Summer is fled ; we may not stay.
Summer is gone.   Good-by ! good-by ! "

WHAT THE ANGEL SAID.

THEY sat in the cool of the day to rest, —
Adam and Eve, and a nameless guest.
The sky o'er the desert was hot and red,
But the palm boughs nestled overhead,
And the bubbling waters of the well
Up and down in their basin fell,
And the goats and the camels browsed at ease,
And the confident song birds sang and flew
In the shade of the thick mimosa trees;
For fear was not when the world was new.

In the early dawning had come the guest,
And whether from east or whether from west
They knew not, nor asked, as he stood and bent
At the entrance of the lowly tent:
He had dipped his hand in the bowl of food,
He had thanked and praised and called it good;

And now between his hosts he sat,
  "And talked of matters so deep and wise
That Eve looked up from her braiding mat
  With wonderment in her beautiful eyes.

" All is not lost," the stranger said,
" Though the garden of God be forfeited ;
Still is there hope for the life of man,
Still can he struggle and will and plan,
Still can he strain toward the shining goal
Which tempts and beckons his sinewy soul ;
Still there is work to brace his thews,
  And love to sweeten the hard-won way,
And the power to give, and the right to choose, —
  And — " He paused ; and the rest he did not say.

Then silence fell, for their thoughts were full
Of the fair lost garden beautiful ;
A homesick silence, which neither broke
Till once again the stranger spoke :
" You are strong," he said, " with the strength of heaven
And the world and its creatures to you are given ;
You shall win in the fight, though many oppose.
  You shall tread on the young of the lion's den,

And the desert shall blossom as the rose
'Neath your tendance." And Adam asked : " And
then ? "

" Then, ripening with the riper age,
Your sons, a goodly heritage,
Like palm-trees in their stately strength,
Shall win to man's estate at length.
Beside thee shall they take their stand,
To do thy will, uphold thy hand,
To speed thy errands with eager feet,
To quit them in their lot like men,
With tendance and obedience meet."
Then once more Adam said, " And then?"

" Then, as mild age draws slowly on,
And faintly burns thy westering sun,
When on the pulse no longer hot
Falls quietude which youth knows not,
When patience rules the tempered will,
And strength is won by sitting still,
Then shall a new-born pleasure come
Into thy heart and arms again,
As children's children fill thy home."
Eve smiled ; but Adam said, " And then?"

"Then " — and the guest rose up to go —
" The best, the last thing shalt thou know :
This life of struggle and of fight
Shall vanish like a wind-blown light ;
And after brief eclipse shall be
Re-lit, to burn more gloriously.
Men by a strange, sad name shall call
   The darkness, and with bated breath
Confront it, but of God's gifts all
   Are nothing worth compared with death."

Even as he spoke his visage gleamed
With light unearthly, and it seemed
That radiant wings, unseen till then,
Lifted and bore him from their ken.
Awe-struck the solitary two
Beheld him vanish from their view.
" It was the angel of the Lord,"
   They said. " How blind we were and dull !
He did not bear the fiery sword ;
   Surely the Lord is pitiful."

And then ? The unrelenting years
Surged tide-like on, with hopes and fears

And labors full, but nevermore
Brought any angel to their door.
But still his words within her heart
Eve kept, and pondered them apart.
And when one fatal day they brought
  Her Abel to her, cold and dead,
She stayed her anguish with this thought:
  " 'T is God's best gift, the angel said."

COMMONPLACE.

"COMMONPLACE life," we say, and we sigh ;
  But why should we sigh as we say? ·
The commonplace sun in the commonplace
  sky,
  Makes up the commonplace day ;
The moon and the stars are commonplace things,
And the flower that blooms, and the bird that sings :
But dark were the world and sad our lot
If the flowers failed and the sun shone not ;
And God, who studies each separate soul,
· Out of commonplace lives makes his beautiful whole.

GOLD, FRANKINCENSE, AND MYRRH.

OLD, frankincense, and myrrh they brought the
new-born Christ, —
Those wise men from the East, — and in the
ox's stall
The far-brought precious gifts they heaped, with love
unpriced;
And Christ the babe looked on, and wondered not at
all.

Gold, frankincense, and myrrh I, too, would offer thee,
 O King of faithful hearts, upon thy Christmas Day;
And poor and little worth although the offering be,
 Because thou art so kind, I dare to think I may.

I bring the gold of faith, which, through the centuries
long,
 Still seeks the Holy Child, and worships at his feet,
And owns him for its Lord, with gladness deep and strong,
 And joins the angel choir, singing in chorus sweet.

The frankincense I bear is worship which can rise,
    Like perfume floating up higher and higher still,
Till on the wings of prayer it finds the far blue skies,
    And falls, as falls the dew, to freshen heart and will.

And last I bring the myrrh, half bitter and half sweet,
    Of my own selfish heart, through sacrifice made clean,
And break the vase and spill the oil upon thy feet,
    O Lord of Christmas Day, as did the Magdalene.

Gold, frankincense, and myrrh, — 't is all I have to bring
    To thee, O Holy Child, now throned in heaven's mid !
Because thou art so kind, take the poor offering,
    And let me go forth blessed, as once the Wise Men did.

A THOUGHT.

GOD, in his power, keeps making more men,
Peopling the great world again and again;
Age after age, as the centuries roll,
Never he makes a mistake with a soul,
Never neglects them, and never forgets.
Atoms in space from their birth to their end,
Dead or alive, he is always their friend.

Those who lived first, when the world was all new,
Still are as dear in his sight as are you;
Perished their names from the earth that they trod,
But every name is remembered by God, —
All that they sought for, and all that they wrought.
Fixed in unlikeness each separate soul,
Brethren and kin in the infinite whole.

Is God not tired, though almighty He is,
As the long years form the slow centuries,
And the slow centuries linked in embrace
Make up the cycles and meet into space?

Wearies He never, nor ceaseth His toil,
Nor says, " It is finished ; creation is done "? —
Men are so many, and God is but one !

Foolish and childish the thought that I frame.
Meteors fall in, but the sun is the same.
What are the birds to the air-spaces free?
What are the fish to the surge or the sea,
Grains to the desert sands, motes to the beam?
Time hides its face at Eternity's call ;
Men may be many, but God he is all.

AT FLOOD.

ALL winter long it ebbed and ebbed, and left the
cold earth bare.
No pulse of growth the bare boughs stirred, no
hope the frozen air;
No twitters cheered the snow-heaped nests, no songs the
vine and trees,
As outward, outward swept the tide, and left the world to
freeze.

Then came a subtle change, — a time when for a mo-
ment's space
Life seemed to stay its flying feet and cease its outward
race,
And, poised as waves poise, turn its face toward the de-
serted shore,
And with a pitying rush come back to visit it once more.

We saw the freshening forces rise in every yellowing
       stem,
In budding oak and tasselled larch and scarlet maple gem.
Inch after inch, wave following wave, it rose on every side ;
And now the tide is at its flood, the blessed summer-tide.

For every ebb there comes a flow ; brave hearts can smile
       at both.
The waters come, the waters go ; we watch them, nothing
       loath.
Led by a hand invisible, their bright waves seem to sing,
" The Lord who rules the winter is the Lord who sends
       the spring ! "

THE ANGELS.

ARE the angels never impatient
    That we are so weak and slow,
    So dull to their guiding touches,
So deaf to the whispers low
With which, entreating and urging,
    They follow us as we go?

Ah no! the pitiful angels
    Are clearer of sight than we,
And they note not only the thing that we are,
    But the thing that we fain would be, —
The hint of gold in the cumbering dross,
    Of fruit on the bare, cold tree.

And I think that at times the angels
    Must smile as mothers smile
At the peevish babies on their knees,
    Loving them all the while,
And cheating the little ones of their pain
    With sweet and motherly wile.

And if they are so patient, the angels,
  How tenderer far than they
Must the mighty Lord of the angels be,
  Whom the heavenly hosts obey,
Who speeds them forth on their errands,
  And cares for us more than they !

NOT YET.

"NOT yet," she cried, "not yet!
  It is the dawning, and life looks so fair;
    Give me my little hour of sun and dew.
  Is it a sin that I should crave my share,
  The common sunshine and the common air,
Before I go away, dark shade, with you?
      Not yet!

"Not yet," she cried, "not yet!
  The day is hot, and noon is pulsing strong,
    And every hour is measured by a task;
  There is no time for sighing or for song.
  Leave me a little longer, just so long
As till my work is done, — 't is all I ask.
      Not yet!

"Not yet," she cried, "not yet!
  Nightfall is near, and I am tired and frail;
    Day was too full, now resting-time has come.

Let me sit still and hear the nightingale,
  And see the sunset colors shift and pale,
Before I take the long, hard journey home.
       Not yet ! "

   And to all these in turn,
Comes Death, the unbidden, universal guest,
With deep and urgent meanings in his eyes,
  And poppied flowers upon his brow, his breast,
  Whispering, " Life is good, but I am best ; "
And never a parted soul looks back and cries,
     " Not yet ! "

TO-DAY AND TO-MORROW.

TO-DAY is mine ; I hold it fast,
  Hold it and use it as I may,
Unmindful of the shadow cast
By that dim thing called Yesterday.

To-morrow hovers just before,
  A bright-winged shape, and lures me on,
Till in my zeal to grasp and know her,
  I drop To-day, — and she is gone.

The bright wings captured lose their light :
  To-morrow weeps, and seems to say,
" I am To-day, — ah, hold me tight !
  Erelong I shall be Yesterday."

"THAT WAS THE TRUE LIGHT, THAT LIGHT-
ETH EVERY MAN THAT COMETH INTO THE
WORLD."

THEY spy it from afar,
  The beacon's fiery star,
And storm-tossed birds, by fierce winds buffeted,
    Rally with half-spent force,
    And shape their struggling course
. To where it rears its blazing, beckoning head.

    Faintly the tired wings beat
    That rhythmical repeat
Which was such joy in summer and in sun;
    Glazed are the keen, bright eyes,
    And heave with panting sighs
The soft and plumèd bosoms every one.

    O'er the white, weltering waves,
    Which yawn like empty graves,
Borne on the urgings of the wind, they fly;
    They reach the luring glow,
    They launch and plunge, and lo!
Are dashed upon the glass, and fall and die.

So through the storm and night,
Outwearied with long flight,
Our souls come crowding o'er the angry sea.
In North, in East, in West,
There is no place of rest,
Except, O kindly Light, except with thee.

No cold, unyielding glass
Bars and forbids to pass ;
Thy dear light scorcheth not, nor burns in vain ;
The soul that finds and knows
Such safe and sure repose
Need nevermore go out or roam again.

Ah, steadfast citadel !
Ah, lamp that burns so well
Upon the Rock of Ages, founded true !
Above the angry sea
We urge our flight to thee.
Shine, kindly Light, and guide us safely through !

THE STAR.

T HEY followed the Star the whole night through ;
 As it moved with the midnight they moved too ;
 And cared not whither it led, nor knew,
   Till Christmas Day in the morning.

And just at the dawn in the twilight shade
They came to the stable, and, unafraid,
Saw the Blessed Babe in the manger laid
   On Christmas Day in the morning.

We have followed the Star a whole long year,
And watched its beckon, now faint, now clear,
And it now stands still as we draw anear
   To Christmas Day in the morning.

And just as the wise men did of old,
In the hush of the winter dawning cold,
We come to the stable, and we behold
   The Child on the Christmas morning.

And just as the wise men deemed it meet
To offer him gold and perfumes sweet,
We would lay our gifts at his holy feet, —
   Our gifts on the Christmas morning.

O Babe, once laid in the ox's bed,
With never a pillow for thy head,
Now throned in the highest heavens instead,
   O Lord of the Christmas morning ! —

Because we have known and have loved thy star,
And have followed it long and followed it far,
From the land where the shadows and darkness are,
   To find thee on Christmas morning, —

Accept the gifts that we dare to bring,
Though worthless and poor the offering,
And help our souls to rise and to sing
   In the joy of thy Christmas morning.

HELEN.

THE autumn seems to cry for thee,
　　Best lover of the autumn days !
　Each scarlet-tipped and wine-red tree,
　　Each russet branch and branch of gold,
　Gleams through its veil of shimmering haze,
　　And seeks thee as they sought of old ;
　For all the glory of their dress,
　They wear a look of wistfulness.

In every wood I see thee stand,
　　The ruddy boughs above thy head,
　And heaped in either slender hand
　　The frosted white and amber ferns,
　The sumach's deep, resplendent red,
　　Which like a fiery feather burns,
　And over all, thy happy eyes,
　Shining as clear as autumn skies.

I hear thy call upon the breeze
   Gay as the dancing wind, and sweet,
And underneath the radiant trees,
   O'er lichens gray and darkling moss,
Follow the trace of those light feet
   Which never were at fault or loss,
But, by some forest instinct led,
Knew where to turn and how to tread.

Where art thou, comrade true and tried?
   The woodlands call for thee in vain,
And sadly burns the autumn-tide
   Before my eyes, made dim and blind
By blurring, puzzling mists of pain
   I look before, I look behind ;
Beauty and loss seem everywhere,
And grief and glory fill the air.

Already, in these few short weeks,
   A hundred things I leave unsaid,
Because there is no voice that speaks
   In answer, and no listening ear,
No one to care now thou art dead !
   And month by month, and year by year,
I shall but miss thee more, and go
With half m tho ht untold I know.

I do not think thou hast forgot,
  I know that I shall not forget,
And some day, glad, but wondering not,
  We two shall meet, and face to face,
In still, fair fields unseen as yet,
  Shall talk of each old time and place,
And smile at pain interpreted
By wisdom learned since we were dead.

LUX IN TENEBRIS.

DARK falls the night, withheld the day,
　　Weary we fare perplexed and chill,
　　Led by one little guiding ray
Shining from centuries far away, —
　Good-will and Peace : Peace and Good-will.

The torch of glory pales and wanes,
　The lamp of love must know decease,
But still o'er far Judæan plains
The quenchless star-beam lives and reigns, —
　Peace and Good-will : Good-will and Peace.

And clear to-day as long ago
　The angel-chorus echoes still,
Above the clamor and the throe
Of human passion, human woe, —
　Good-will and Peace : Peace and Good-will.

Through eighteen hundred stormy years
   The dear notes ring, and will not cease ;
And past all mists of mortal tears
The guiding star rebukes our fears, —
   Peace and Good-will : Good-will and Peace.

Shine, blessed star, the night is black,
   Shine, and the heavens with radiance fill,
While on thy slender, guiding track
The angel voices echo back, —
   Good-will and Peace : Peace and Good-will.

LENT.

IS it the Fast which God approves,
  When I awhile for flesh eat fish,
  Changing one dainty dish
For others no less good?

Do angels smile and count it gain
  That I compose my laughing face
  To gravity for a brief space,
Then straightway laugh again?

Does Heaven take pleasure as I sit
  Counting my joys as usurers gold, —
  This bit to give, that to withhold,
Weighing and measuring it ;

Setting off abstinence from dance
  As buying privilege of song ;
  Calling six right and seven wrong,
With decorous countenance ;

Compounding for the dull to-day
　　By projects for to-morrow's fun,
　　Checking off each set task as done,
Grudging a short delay?

I cannot think that God will care
　　For such observance; He can see
　　The very inmost heart of me,
And every secret there.

But' if I keep a truer Lent,
　　Not heeding what I wear or eat,
　　Not balancing the sour with sweet,
Evenly abstinent,

And lay my soul with all its stain
　　Of travel from the year-long road,
　　Between the healing hands of God
To be made clean again;

And put my sordid self away,
　　Forgetting for a little space
　　The petty prize, the eager race,
The restless, striving day;

Opening my darkness to the sun,
  Opening my narrow eyes to see
  The pain and need so close to me
Which I had willed to shun ;

Praying God's quickening grace to show
  The thing he fain would have me do,
  The errand that I may pursue
And quickly rise and go ; —

If so I do it, starving pride,
  Fasting from sin instead of food,
  God will accept such Lent as good,
And bless its Easter-tide.

PALM SUNDAY.

HE multitude was crowding all the way,
            But yesterday,
To see and touch the Lord as he rode by,
            To catch his eye,
Or at the very least a palm-branch fling
Upon the pathway of the chosen King.

Faded and dry those palms lie in the sun,
            Witherèd each one ;
Those glad, rejoicing shouters presently
            Will flock to see,
With never thought of pity or of loss,
The King of Glory on his cruel cross.

Lord, we would fain some little palm-branch lay
            Upon thy way ;
But we have nothing fair enough or sweet
            For holy feet
To tread, nor dare our sin-stained garments fling
Upon the road where rides the Righteous King.

Yet thou, all-gracious One, didst not refuse
Those fickle Jews ;
And even such worthless leaves as we may cull,
Faded and dull,
Thou wilt endure and pardon and receive,
Because thou knowest we have naught else to give.

So, Lord, our stubborn wills we first will break,
If thou wilt take ;
And next our selfishness, and then our pride, —
And what beside ?
Our hearts, Lord, poor and fruitless though they be,
And quick to change, and nothing worth to see.

If but the foldings of thy garment's hem
Shall shadow them,
These worthless leaves which we have brought and strewed
Along thy road
Shall be raised up and made divinely sweet,
And fit to lie beneath thy gracious feet.

SOUL AND BODY.

THE Soul said to the Body, in the watches of the
    night :
    " I am the nobler part of thee, stronger and far
    more worth.
God gave me of his life of life a tiny point of light ;
    I show his glory to the world, but thou art of the earth."

The Body answered to the Soul : " Lower I am, and yet
    God made me in his image for angel eyes to see.
Thou art but viewless essence, whom all men would forget
    Except for the abiding-place which thou hast found in
    me."

The Soul said to the Body : " I guide thee at my will.
    I am the wind within the sail, which else would lifeless
    swing ;
I am the mainspring of the watch, which else, inert and
    still,
    Would cumber all the universe, a dead and useless
    thing."

"I too have rule," the Body cried. "I curb thy higher
  flights ;
  I fetter all thy soarings, and I bind thee, and I grieve.
I can sting thee into wakefulness through long, unresting
  nights ;
  Can take the glory from thy noon, the splendor from
  thy eve."

"And well can I return such wrong," replied the eager
  Soul.
  "How often hast thou laid thee down, to find thy sleep
  denied?
While I quickened in thy brain, robbed thy heart-beats of
  control,
  And poured through every artery my warm, pulsating
  tide?

"Thou shalt lie down to sleep one day, and long that sleep
  shall last,
  For I will shake thy shackles off and soar up to the
  skies ;
What power shall avail thee then to break thy slumber
  fast?
  What voice shall reach thy dreaming ear, to say to thee,
  'Arise'?"

"Ah, Soul!" the Body humbly urged, "be merciful, I
          pray ;
  Thou art the nobler part, but thou canst never let me go.
I have my certain share of all, thy best, thy worst, alway :
  We are inextricably blent.   God willed it should be so.

" Thou wilt reach heaven before me, but I may follow too.
  There is a resurrection for the Body, as the Soul,;
Comrades to all eternity, we should be comrades true
  Who own one common fate and life, who seek the self-
          same goal.

" Forbear, then, to reproach me, O brother given by
          Heaven !
  I wrong myself in wronging thee, dearest and closest
          friend !
Let all our variance and strife be buried and forgiven,
  And let us work together in love unto the end."

Then the Soul smiled on the Body, and the Body drank
          the smile,
  As meadow pastures drink the flood of sunshine still and
          deep ;
And the two embraced each other, and in a little while,
  Close folded in the Body's arms, the Soul had fallen
          asleep.

SOUND AT CORE.

THE wind is fierce and loud and high,
The angry tempest hurtles by;
With quivering keel and straining sail
The ship of State confronts the gale.
Rocks are ahead and peril near;
But still we face the storm, nor fear,
Saying this brave truth o'er and o'er:
"The nation's heart is sound at core."

We knew it in those darker days
When all the kind, familiar ways
And all the tenderness of life
Seemed lost in bitterness and strife;
When, torn with shot and riddled through,
Lay in the dust our Red and Blue,
Dropped by the gallant hands that bore,
"The nation's heart is sound at core."

We said it when the war-cloud rent,
-And out of field and out of tent
The bronzèd soldiers, Blue and Gray,
Took each the peaceful homeward way ;
When the foiled traitors sought to attain
By fraud what force had failed to gain, —
Heart-sick, we said the words once more :
" The nation's heart is sound at core."

And always, as the worst seemed near,
And stout hearts failed for very fear,
Came a great throb the country through, —
The nation's heart still beating true !
Ah, mother-land and mother-breast,
We still will trust you and will rest ;
Although waves howl and tempests lower,
Your heart, our heart, is sound at core.

THE OLD VILLAGE.

T lies among the greenest hills
     New England's depths can show ;
About their base the river fills
And empties as the distant mills
     Control its ebb and flow :
It had a quick life of its own,
     But that was long ago.

Two centuries have rolled away
     Since a small, hardy band
Turned their sad faces from the bay,
The dim sky-line where England lay,
     And boldly marched inland.
Before them lay the wilderness,
     Behind them lay the strand.

Bravely they plunged into the waste
  By white foot never trod ;
Bravely and busily they traced
The village boundaries, and placed
    Their ploughs in virgin sod ;
Built huts, and then a meeting-house
    Where man might worship God.

The huts gave place to houses white ;
    The axe-affrighted woods
Shrank back to left, shrank back to right ;
The valleys laughed with harvest light ;
    The river's vagrant moods
Were curbed by clattering wheels, which shook
    The once green solitudes.

And years flowed on, and life flowed by.
    The hills were named and known.
The young looked out with eager eye
From the " old " village ; by and by
    They stole forth one by one,
Leaving the old folks in their homes
    To labor on alone.

And one by one the old folks died,
  Each in his lonely way.
The doors which once stood open wide,
To let a busy human tide
  Sweep in and out all day,
Were closed ; the unseeing windows stared
  Just as a blind man may.

The mills, abandoned, ceased to whir ;
  The unchecked river ran
Its old-time courses, merrier,
And glad in spirit, as it were,
  For its escape from man,
Teased the dumb wheels, and mocked and played
  As only a river can.

Looking to-day across the space,
  Beyond the flower-fringed track
Which once was road, the eye can trace
The outlines of a cellar-place,
  A half-burned chimney-back :
They mark the ruins of a home
  Now empty, cold, and black.

And here and there an old dame stands
   Some farm-house window nigh,
Or, dark against the pasture-lands,
A ploughman old, with trembling hands,
   Checks his team suddenly,
And turns a gray head to the road
   To watch the passer-by.

Above the empty village lies
   One thickly peopled spot,
Where gray stones in gray silence rise,
And tell to sunset and sunrise
   Of past lives that are not, —
The lives that fought and strove and toiled
   And builded.   And for what?

'T is Nature's law in everything.
   The river seeks the sea ;
But not one droplet wandering
Goes ever back to feed the spring.
   Such things are and must be.
The gone is gone, the lost is lost,
   Fled irrevocably.

Old village on the lonely hill,
  Deserted by your own,
Your spended lifelike mountain rill
Has gone to swell the tide and fill
  Some sea unseen, unknown.
Let this brave thought your comfort be,
  As thus you die alone.

A GREETING.

H, dear and friendly Death,
   End of my road, however long it be,
   Waiting with hospitable hands stretched out
     And full of gifts for me !

   Why do we call thee foe,
Clouding with darksome.mists thy face divine?
Life, she was sweet, but poor her largess seems
     When matched with thine.

   Thy amaranthine blooms
Are not less lovely than her rose of joy ;
And the rare, subtle perfumes which they breathe
     Never the senses cloy.

   Thou holdest in thy store
Full satisfaction of all doubt, reply
To question, and the golden clews to dreams
     Which idly passed us by.

Darkness to tired eyes,
Perplexed with vision, blinded with long day;
Quiet to busy hands, glad to fold up
    And lay their work away.

A balm for anguish past,
Rest to the long unrest which smiles did hide;
The recognitions thirsted for in vain,
    And still by life denied.

A nearness, all unknown
While in these stifling, prisoning bodies pent,
Unto thy soul and mine, beloved, made one
    At last in full content.

Thou bringest me mine own,
The garnered flowers which felt thy sickle keen,
And the full vision of that Face divine,
    Which I have loved unseen.

Oh, dear and friendly Death,
End of my road, however long it be,
Nearing me day by day, I still can smile
    Whene'er I think of thee !

CHANGELESS.

E say, "The sun has set," and we sorrow sore
As we watch the darkness creep the landscape
o'er,
And the thick shadows fall, and the night draw on ;
And we mourn for the brightness lost, and the vanished sun.

And all the time the sun in the self-same place
Waits, ready to clasp the earth in his embrace,
Ready to give to all of his stintless ray ;
And 'tis we who have " set," it is we who have turned away !

" The Lord has hidden his face," we sadly cry,
As we sit in the night of grief with no helper by.
" Guiding uncounted worlds in their courses dim,
How should our little pain be marked by him?"

But all the while that we mourn, the Lord stands near,
And the Son divine is waiting to help and hear ;
And 't is we who hide our faces, and blindly turn away,
While the Sun of the soul shines on mid the perfect day.

EASTER.

FLOWERS die not in the winter-tide,
   Although they wake in spring;
   Pillowed 'neath mounds of fleecy snow,
While skies are gray and storm-winds blow,
   All patiently they bide,
Fettered by frost, and bravely wait,
And trust in spring or soon or late.

Hope dies not in the winter-tide,
   Though sore it longs for spring;
Cool morn may ripen to hot noon,
And evening dusks creep all too soon
   The noonday sun to hide;
But through the night there stir and thrill
The sleeping strengths of life and will.

For souls there comes a winter-tide,
  For souls there blooms a spring ;
Though winter days may linger long,
And snows be deep and frosts be strong,
  And faith be sorely tried,
When Christ shall shine, who is the Sun,
Spring-time shall be for every one.

Oh, mighty Lord of winter-tide !
  Oh, loving Lord of spring !
Come to our hearts this Easter Day,
Melt all the prisoning ice away,
  And evermore abide,
Making both good and ill to be
Thy blessed opportunity.

THE WORLD IS VAST.

THE world is vast and we are small,
    We are so weak and it so strong,
        Onward it goes, nor cares at all
For us, — our silence or our song,
Our fast-day or our festival.

    We tremble as we feel it sway
Beneath our feet as on we fare ;
    But, like a ball which children play,
God spins it through the far blue air.
We are his own ; why should we care?

University Press: John Wilson & Son, Cambridge.